One First Love
THE LETTERS OF ELLEN LOUISA TUCKER
TO
RALPH WALDO EMERSON

One First Love

THE LETTERS OF
ELLEN LOUISA TUCKER
TO
RALPH WALDO EMERSON

EDITED BY
Edith W. Gregg

THE BELKNAP PRESS OF
HARVARD UNIVERSITY PRESS
CAMBRIDGE · MASSACHUSETTS
1962

© 1962 BY THE PRESIDENT AND FELLOWS OF HARVARD COLLEGE
ALL RIGHTS RESERVED

DISTRIBUTED IN GREAT BRITAIN BY
OXFORD UNIVERSITY PRESS
LONDON

TYPOGRAPHY BY BURTON J JONES JR

PRINTED AT THE HARVARD UNIVERSITY PRINTING OFFICE
CAMBRIDGE, MASSACHUSETTS, U.S.A.

BOUND BY STANHOPE BINDERY, BOSTON, MASSACHUSETTS

LIBRARY OF CONGRESS CATALOG CARD NUMBER 62-19215

Preface

After the death of Ralph Waldo Emerson's daughter, Edith Emerson Forbes, in 1929, and of his son, Edward Waldo, in 1930, the Ralph Waldo Emerson Memorial Association was formed for the purpose of maintaining interest in the literary works of Emerson, and to preserve his library and manuscripts. The interest in his thought and writing has been increasing, and by now nearly every word that he wrote has been published or is being worked on by scholars for publication. All of his letters, his notes and journals, his sermons and lectures, letters to him and about him, have been available to interested people.

A conspicuous omission is noticeable in this mass of material. One of the profound influences in Emerson's life was his love for his first wife, Ellen. She came into his life as a great radiance, and the memory of this first love never left him. We have only glimpsed the reflection of this radiance in his journals and letters but have had no direct evidence of it, as nothing of Ellen's thought or writing has been available. Her letters had been kept together and were slightly charred when the Emerson house in Concord caught fire in 1872. They came into the possession of Emerson's children, but were considered as sacred treasures, and too personal for general reading or publication. There has been a gap, therefore, in any

PREFACE

understanding of the period of Emerson's life when Ellen was playing so large a part in it.

The R.W.E. Memorial Association, which has held these letters since 1930, feels that it is time to make them available for general reading and to have Ellen speak for herself through them. The picture is not complete; there must have been many other letters from her and about her. From this small group, however, which are printed in their entirety, can be drawn the outline of an unusual and beautiful person, whose influence was to last very much longer than her own life.

As a member of the R.W.E. Memorial Association, I was given the opportunity to work on the letters and the small amount of other material that could be located. The original plan was merely to print Ellen's letters to Emerson. In going over the material I found letters to Aunt Mary, Aunt Hubbard, etc., and bits that Ellen had written in Emerson's letters to his brothers. A rhymed and humorous description of a journey to Philadelphia seemed an interesting addition to supplement the letters. A selection of Ellen's verses, about half of those Emerson chose to copy into his notebook, was necessary to round out the picture. A few quotations from her notebooks have been put in, either because they throw light on her character or because they clarify aspects of the letters.

Much more might be done in building up the picture of Ellen's life in Concord, New Hampshire, and in further genealogical research. The Tucker

PREFACE

and Kent families were an interesting group; I was tempted to add more about them. Not all the people mentioned in the letters have been identified, and I have preferred not to guess; the identities do not seem vital to an appreciation of the letters. Some of the young men were probably students, other people were neighbors or casual acquaintances.

I have tried to keep the emphasis entirely on Ellen, and have omitted any discussion of Emerson's work and importance. I have identified members of his family only briefly. There are many books about every aspect of Emerson's life and work that can be read for a fuller knowledge of the background. His collected letters are available, and are interesting to read in connection with Ellen's. His poems, essays, and sermons are in print, and the complete journals of this period will shortly be published.

We do not have Emerson's letters to Ellen, nor letters to or from members of her family. If we did, the obscure bits in her letters would doubtless be clear. There are places where the writing is plain but the sense is not. There are obscure allusions, and a great many quotations, some of which are not readily identifiable. The Bible is quoted frequently, and she was also familiar with many hymns and the popular songs of the day. She read gift-books and annuals, collections of verse, the works of modern poets like Southey, Scott, Bryant, and Mrs. Hemans, and older poets like Herbert and Young. Emerson's early poems she knew well. She had read more philosophical and

PREFACE

religious books than novels. Whenever possible I have traced the quotations, since they give the only clue to her reading and education.

The only book of hers that seems to have survived is her *Sabbath Recreations*. This book, her notebooks and album, and her letters are the property of the R.W.E. Memorial Association. Some of the material is in the Houghton Library of Harvard University, some still held by the Association.

Ellen's memory was honored by Emerson's second wife, Lydia, and by Lydia's daughter Edith, my grandmother. It was a memory of charm and courage. In his journal some years after her death, Emerson says his life is not a chasm, "so brilliantly sometimes the vision of Ellen's beauty and love and life come out of the darkness." These letters may bring her enough into the light for us to catch a faint glimpse of that vision.

EDITH EMERSON WEBSTER GREGG

Contents

INTRODUCTION

1

PART ONE

DECEMBER 1828 — SEPTEMBER 1829

11

PART TWO

DECEMBER 1829 — FEBRUARY 1831

111

PART THREE

POEMS AND NOTEBOOKS

147

NOTES 171

NOTES ON THE TEXT 203

INDEX 207

Illustrations

Following page 20

Bezaleel Tucker. From an oil painting done before 1820. Artist unknown.

Ellen Louisa Tucker. From a photograph of the original miniature painted by Sarah Goodridge, spring 1829.

Ralph Waldo Emerson. From a photograph of the miniature painted by Sarah Goodridge, spring 1829.

Margaret Tucker Kent. From the oil painting by Henry Cheever Pratt, summer 1829.

Following page 52

Letter 6, written in Derry but mailed in Concord, New Hampshire, on May 22, 1829.

Last page of Letter 23, apparently written on July 23 or 24, 1829.

Following page 68

Last page of Letter 25, written on July 27, 1829.

Letter 36, written on September 18, 1829.

Introduction

THESE letters were written by a girl of seventeen to a young minister who was wondering whether to settle down as a Unitarian preacher at Boston's Second Church. He was twenty-five and had been living in Cambridge, preaching in towns around Boston when invited to substitute for a regular minister. He had preached for three Sundays in Concord, New Hampshire, just a year earlier, in December 1827 and January 1828. In a notebook called "Autobiography," where he listed his preaching engagements and trips, there is the brief note "Dec. 25th [1827] Saw Ellen L. Tucker." He had been back again to preach in May and June of 1828. Although he had written nothing in his letters or journals to indicate an interest in Ellen, the invitation from the Unitarian group in Concord to return in December 1828 must have been a welcome one to Ralph Waldo Emerson. His brother Edward had not been well, and went along with him for the trip and a change of scene. They were in Concord on December 6th, Waldo carrying with him a gift for Ellen, a book called *Forget me not*. The only entry in "Autobiography" for December was on the seventeenth — "I was engaged to Ellen Louisa Tucker."

A week later he announced his engagement to his older brother William. "It is now just a year since I

INTRODUCTION

became acquainted with Ellen," he wrote, "but I thought I had got over my blushes & wishes when now I determined to go into that dangerous neighborhood again on Edward's account. But the presumptuous man was overthrown by the eye & the ear & surrendered at discretion."

Ellen's father, Bezaleel Tucker, a prosperous Boston merchant, had died in 1820, and four years later her mother had married Colonel William Austin Kent, a prominent citizen of Concord, New Hampshire, whose first wife had died some years earlier. Ellen and her older sisters Margaret and Paulina were living in Concord with their mother and stepfather. There was a family history of pulmonary tuberculosis: George, the oldest, had died in Paris while traveling for his health, and a sister Mary had died young. Ellen had frequent sick spells. She was deeply religious, and she had time during sickness and convalescence to develop her philosophy. She wrote in her early notebook: "People say to me – well if you have riches you have sickness – meaning I am not so much better off than they who though poor yet are blessed in it with robust frames and eat the bread of labour with the salt of health – Nay now – I often think instead of calling sickness the counterbalance of good – that I should be glad of its visitations – for they come as blessings, they are necessary to the health of my soul —— 'Tis perhaps grievous for a while to be pained and eaten up with bodily sickness – but every pain is a scourge to the old sins that lurk within and

INTRODUCTION

under the paleness of the frame the soul has a roseate cheek – the graces flourish and God bends over our pillow and we are in the stillness of the cease of worldly toil gradually becoming more and more perfect as He who is in heaven is perfect." She wanted to write, however, and she did regret that her poor health interfered with her development as a poet. "God has given me a harp," she wrote, "and the strings I believe are sound and sweet but the part which holds them the bridge the fretts are weak and wasting — Every day I ought to get one drop from my brain of clear distilled essence – I ought – but ah!! ——" She studied religious and philosophical books, read and wrote very solemn poetry; but this serious side was counterbalanced by the gay and sociable tendency of her nature. She called these two aspects Lady Frolick and Lady Penseroso, and was well aware of her varying moods. In an epigram in one of her notebooks she makes her Muse address her thus:

"Poor straining wretch, and can't you make a verse
About a barn, a ball-room, or a hearse?
Fain would I help thee but I always fail
To squeeze out *sense* – where nonsense will prevail – "

Whenever her health was good she led a gay life. There were rides, drives, music parties, callers, visitors, excursions to the country. Ellen was interested in clothes and fashions. She wore the latest thing in sleeves, and had her hair curled in a fashionable man-

INTRODUCTION

ner. It must have been a lively household, since Mary Jane and Rebecca, Colonel Kent's daughters by his first wife, as well as Margaret, Paulina, and Ellen Tucker, lived at home. His sons William and George lived in Concord, and Edward came to visit. The young Kents and Tuckers seem to have been happy together, and Colonel Kent was devoted to his wife and stepdaughters. There were family pets — the spaniel Byron, white mice, squirrels, a canary, and the riding and driving horses. It was a hospitable house; visitors were welcome, and Waldo Emerson had been greeted with cordiality as a visiting preacher, then with affection as a suitor of Ellen's. Their engagement apparently met with happy approval. In the letter to William announcing it, Emerson says that he is "as happy as it is safe in life to be in the affection of the lady & the approbation of the friends."

It is tantalizing that no letters written by Emerson to Ellen have survived. At first he had been uneasy about having his letters kept, and she offered to burn them. He did not insist on this; she later mentions one of his letters "reposing among its fellows." There was also an attempt to correspond in French, presumably for fear someone else should read their letters: Ellen refers to a "Gallic veil." It seems probable that Ellen treasured Waldo's letters during her lifetime, and that Waldo destroyed them himself after her death. It is fortunate that Ellen's letters did survive, as except for them, and for four notebooks containing verses and bits of prose, we have nothing tangible

INTRODUCTION

left to tell us of her charm. Her "magick spell" seems to have fallen on everybody who knew her, not only on the young preacher, who says "she is very beautiful by universal consent." In January 1829 he tried to describe her to William: "Well then she is perfectly simple though very elegant in her manners; then she has common sense; then she has imagination & knows the difference between good poetry & bad; then she makes fine verses herself, then she is good, — & has character enough to be religious, then she is beautiful, & finally I love her. If my story is short, it is true." Waldo's other brother, Charles, who must have been talking to Edward, reported in a New Year's letter to their Aunt Mary: "Ellen is, we understand, for we do not see her till next week, a beautiful, sensible, religious girl. She is rich too. Though this seems forgotten in her loveliness and excellence."

The only picture of her is a miniature painted in the spring of 1829. She gave it to Waldo, who was so anxious for William to see what she looked like that he offered to lend him the miniature: "the rather may I miss it for a week," he says, "because 'tis a very imperfect copy of her face, & is so judged by those who know her much less nearly than I & yet have seen her much — Still 'tis a copy & so wd. be better to you than none at all." He gave her a miniature of himself in a red morocco case, which was probably a better likeness, though she speaks of its "foreboding expression."

At the time most of these letters were written,

INTRODUCTION

Waldo's widowed mother, Ruth Haskins Emerson, was living in Concord, Massachusetts, with Phebe and Ezra Ripley, her husband's mother and stepfather. The letters refer to "Aunt Mary," the interesting and formidable Mary Moody Emerson, Waldo's severe and loving critic. Ellen met Waldo's brother Edward in December 1828, and Charles after her family moved to Boston. His brother William was a lawyer in New York; Charles was teaching school; and Edward, who had recovered from a nervous breakdown, was studying law.

The letters have been copied as they were written, with the original spellings and abbreviations. Some words are missing, either at the edges where the paper is charred or blurred, or where the seal has torn off a bit of the paper. Except for the first one, the letters are addressed to the "Rev. R. Waldo Emerson, Boston, Mass." Most of them are undated, so that the endorsement written by Emerson, which is in brackets at the head of each letter, is often the only indication, aside from the contents, as to the date. The dates on the postmarks, in faint red ink, are frequently illegible. Some were not postmarked, but were carried to Boston by Colonel Kent, or by some other messenger.

Since Waldo's letters to Ellen have apparently been destroyed, nothing remains to represent his side of the correspondence except the poems, included here, which he sent or gave to her. Most of these appear scattered through his journals, beginning with the

INTRODUCTION

first: "All that thy virgin soul can ask, beautiful Ellen —." The dates when she received them cannot be ascertained exactly, but the chronology is clear. The unfinished fragment "And do I waste my time" is written on a scrap of paper tucked into one of Ellen's notebooks. "I am alone. Sad is my solitude" was copied by Waldo at the end of the notebook containing her verses. These two have not heretofore been published.

Ellen's first letter is postmarked "Concord N.H. Dec. 29" and is addressed to "Rev. R. Waldo Emerson, Cambridge, Mass."

PART ONE

DECEMBER 1 8 2 8 — SEPTEMBER 1 8 2 9

[1] (*Dec 1828*)

Dear Waldo
 I am resolved to night to let you peep into the deep well of my heart which is bubbling up with a crowd of newly arrived thoughts each pressing for an outlet but some more importunate than others will by their continual coming weary me therefore I shall give them speedy utterance. Oh naughty naughty that you are – that you will not spare me a blush. Do you require me to confess in so many words that I love you? And if you did should I have made that confession unsought and unbidden? It vexes me sadly that you should think me capable of encouraging your affectionate attentions toward me without any reason — it would be dishonorably trifling with the deepest feelings of your heart —— Yet if you still require it and are determined to humble this proud spirit – I will whisper something into the ear of your heart which will reassure you — Why was it that long ago while supplicating God in behalf of my nearest and dearest friends that I could not cease untill I had asked a blessing to rest upon "one *whom* I *loved*" —— Oh I never thought that I should draw aside the veil thus from the sacred places of my soul – but I am rejoiced that I must *write* it – and you need not imagine me very *rosy* now for my cheek feels as pale as the paper upon which I am writing. I have been

thus far through life a solitary thing I mean as it respects intercourse with those of my own age and standing – therefore I have had no confidents. My father and mother I should not expect to enter into all my youthful friendships and loves The frosts of age (Oh the metaphorical droppings of a girl in her teens) have chilled the swift flowing fount of youthful passion – and it has yielded to the slower smoother stream of parental solicitude A brother and a sister have that in their hearts which will answer to each other, a sort of sympathetic chord. *My* sisters have been always apart from me – hence they have been ignorant of things which I dared not commit to paper — and these have been few — So you now know how far to put yourself in my power and do not believe that a woman is incapable of keeping a secret —— Did you ever think of the strange sort of restraint that existed between us when you were here? Or were you unconscious of it —— I have just bethought myself that to me alone it might have been troublesome. I can only account for it in the same manner in which I accounted for the immoveability of my tongue in your presence —— My thoughts from long seclusion had grown timid — and though they would often fly to my lips yet when the door opened they were so alarmed that they fled for dear life to hide themselves. If you had watched Waldo you would often have seen them fly from the door to the windows or have caught them peeping forth. (very clearly expressed)
    Your mother — how I long to see her   I shall take

pride in telling her what a good mother God has already given me and should she chance to like me or love me as I am resolved she must — how happy I shall be. For the breathings of so many affectionate ♡s can not fail to blow all life's clouds away or at least to gild them if they are immoveable —— I hope I shall answer her expectations and desires —— I am glad that you have seen my sisters – and I do not fear but you will like them better on a longer acquaintance. What letter is Margaret to show you? And that little note too which was not intended for your eye – I am glad I said so little about you because you had the impudence to steal it ——

Every day I read in Charles 5th and I like it much — it is a torment to me that you recommended it — for no sooner do I take it up and fix my eye on its long pages than a great *long nose* (verily like the shadow of my own when the sun is low) presents itself and thwarts every attempt which I make to think only of the *Emperor Charles 5th* I have been reviving some old French words in my head I find want of practice has put them asleep but they walk drowsily forth and I doubt not I can catch the idea of anything you chuse to write. If it takes more of your precious time to write in this way I would not. Locks and keys form a barrier as impenetrable as a Gallic veil – still faithless – write and after I have graved it on memory's yielding tablet I will commit the copy to the flames. Your "tinkling ryhmes" I love to read — write me some more when you can —— *My* muse is a disobedient lady and loves not the cold though a week ago last Wednesday night she smiled faintly upon me — perhap one day you shall see the product.

I have been all day to hear Mr Cole – and have had a great deal of real enjoyment in the solitude of my little chamber — God has been merciful and kind to me during the past year. How prone are we though constant recipients of his bounty to forget the provident hand and the tender care of the Good Sheperd of our souls   to revel in his sweetest pastures unthankfully – How little have we endured   how small have been our trials compared to some who have been forced to drink deep of the cup of affliction with nothing to cheer them but the glistenings ever and anon of the "pearl of great price" at the bottom (matronly reflections) —— But you must weary of my feebly expressed thoughts – which I am afraid are losing too much of their timidity ——

One thing I must tell you – that Mrs Birch's fluttering spirit which has been so long on the wing has at last fled for aye —— Poor Weston fails daily —— Good night – they are calling me ——

Monday Morn — Good morrow – I was called away last night to see *little* John Williams who has caused me great compunction of conscience by presenting me with a beautiful lithograph head of Pres Kirkland which you have probably seen — the little man heaps coals of fire upon my head – by returning me thus attention for neglect ——

One week from next Friday is the day appointed

1828

for a trip to the city — I anticipate it with delight – and hope Boston air and smart smiling Boston phizzes will do wonders for Mother – who is a little better than when you were here

Will you remember me to your brother Edward and tell him I am to take my first lesson in skating the next day that Old Sol shows his smiling face   with Miss Sparhawk — be not surprised if you hear of broken heads ——

Brother Edward   wife and darling are now with us – Edward regrets that he came too late to see you and has told me a great deal about you – your poetical talent   fine disposition etc. ——

I grieve to have made so many blurs and blunders in this epistle because it will take you longer to read it — I know they were unavoidable and it would be quite out of character for me to write a faultless letter ——

You have no little green covered book to say to you "Forget me not"   but then you have a "Token" & a "Talisman" in the love of a faithful ♡ ——

        Ellen T —— Ah fate cannot etc.

On his return to Boston after he had become engaged, R.W.E. wrote in his journal the first of his poems about Ellen:

TO ELLEN

All that thy virgin soul can ask be thine,
Beautiful Ellen, — let this prayer be mine.
The first devotion that my soul has paid
To mortal grace it pays to thee, fair maid.
I am enamoured of thy loveliness,
Lovesick with thy sweet beauty, which shall bless
With its glad light my path of life around,
Which now is joyless where thou art not found.
Now am I stricken with the sympathy
That binds the whole world in electric tie;
I hail love's birth within my hermit breast,
And welcome the bright ordinance to be blest.
I was a hermit whom the lone Muse cheers,
I sped apart my solitary years,
I found no joy in woman's meaning eye
When Fashion's merry mob were dancing by;
Yet had I read the law all laws above,
Great Nature hath ordained the heart to love;
Yet had I heard that in this mortal state
To every mind exists its natural mate;
That God at first did marry soul to soul,
Though lands divide and seas between them roll.
Then eagerly I searched each circle round,
I panted for my mate, but no mate found.

I saw bright eyes, fair forms, complexions fine,
But not a single soul that spoke to mine.
At last the star broke through the hiding cloud,
At last I found thee in the silken crowd;
I found thee, Ellen, born to love and shine,
And I who found am blessed to call thee mine.

There seems to have been time for only one letter before the Kent household moved to a boarding house in Boston for the rest of the winter. Emerson moved into Boston also, boarding with his friend Abel Adams in Chardon Street, and in January he received a call to the Second Church to take the place of the Reverend Henry Ware. He accepted the position and was ordained in March. He was able to spend a good deal of time with Ellen until the end of April, when her family took a trip to Worcester and Hartford. In May they moved back to New Hampshire, and Ellen began to write regularly.

[2]   (*Worcester, 1 May 1829*)
Worcester – Thursday

My dear Waldo

Your letter was better than all the empty parting kisses in the world   and though some did wonder why I did not poke my hand out the window to give a parting shake   you I well know did not —— What a blessed thing is this silent mutual understanding! It lifts us above the ordinary ceremonies and a shake of the hand at such a time is a mockery of the depth of the feelings —— I wish I had 3 lives   I do not like such furious gaiety – neither do I fancy such lackadaisical pensiveness —— But I would acquire – a cheerful   yes   cheerful is the word – a cheerful heart – able to laugh when occasion requires and stop when the cause ceaseth — to be grave – & not depressed – I hate a foreboding temper ——

It never occurred to me that I should be so really and almost sinfully impatient to see you before I had been absent 3 or 4 days but – tell it not in Gath that

1829

I have counted the days over & over – the suns that must rise & set before I am with you – 40 miles is a wide wide space – and it is not always sufficient that the 7 league boots of the heart will travel it o'er so easily   for it makes such long visits that it leaves my body a perfect nut-shell – and I with a vacant stare sit upright, looking like an Egyptian mummy or a stranger spirit — this is another sort of life which I have begun to live   or rather an intellectual death I have begun ——

Speaking of these again – I will say that Lady Frolick seldom pays me such sort of visits as those of the last 2 or 3 days and oh Waldo if you knew me — you would ken why on that occasion I chose to invite Lady Frolick to spend those last days with me and why I insisted on her bringing all her budgets into the closets of my heart and crowding them to overflowing   I looked into your eyes when you said "Ellen lives 2 lives"   and wished I might expel my visitor a while without fear of the Lady Penseroso with her *overwhelming* weakness who had long been watching an opportunity to slip in   It could not have pleased you greatly to have seen me then so extremely gay – and the other I harbour but seldom to tarry long ——
The currents flowed both ways so strongly that no bridge of indifference could be built — and of the least of 2 evils – natural & best is it that we choose the least harmful to *ourselves* & others ——

I cannot help building fairy castles for next summer and I place myself as their mistress – strong to endure all that may be laid upon myself and able to assist in lightening the burdens of the weaker —— Should all these prove little better than the fairy frostwork of last January ——— If I may but enjoy beneath their ruins one little part of the peace and joy that I did last winter   I am rich in pleasures ——

When I get into Dr Jackson's "house not made with hands" in the apple tree – then will be a fine time to write sermons for the Boston pulpit – I fear the parishioners would talk faster than ever of *departed* Ware – and complain bitterly of the miserable food they recieved from the sheperd who had heretofore fed them so luxuriously – of the prematureness of his *second* childhood. Even little Johny Williams might look at the shoes with a reasonable hope of preference when the last toe was withdrawn ——

I wonder much if ever engaged Miss recieved such loveletters as I do — so thoroughly good to my heart so renewing so strengthing, so – I would not *say* this to you but I cannot help feeling that I am favored among women every day that I live – and know you more – and I *do* repose entire confidence in you – although I withold oftentimes the paper darkened by the *philosophical* wisdom and the deep *reason* of the every day effusions of my brain – and show you the astonishing Sabbaday productions only —— But as to this why should I when I see such real folly let it live   As to yourself   26 years have done much for you — and your *writings* have all a deep shade of sense — and if you were only 17 perhaps they would

BEZALEEL TUCKER

ELLEN LOUISA TUCKER

RALPH WALDO EMERSON

MARGARET TUCKER KENT

1829

have the shade too – though at 26 if I live shall I not marvel that I condescend to catch any of the little stragglers of my imagination and pin them to paper? – Not that I expect Oh King to exceed the Queen of Sheba – or surpass Solomon – But I humbly trust that "Each day that I live I may in a measure correct the follies of the past" —— And friend Waldo we love each other – this shall be our beautiful peace spirit And though my progress be slow in earthly lore yet I know each day that I love as I do now brings me more gratefully near to Heaven and enobles me to a higher purer worship ——

Lady Penseroso thinks she has done already more than you required of her —— Lady Frolick – would if you please take lessons in moderation – before she presume to teach —— They are however both at your service and hope to be more sweetly blended ere they shall again appear before his Ldship – P & M were delighted with Gra*m*pa's good will ——

The vespers aye & the matins are earnest & constant – and truly am I yours dear Waldo

[3] (*Hartford, May, 1829*)
(*Ellen Tucker*)
Hartford – Monday

Dear Waldo

We have just arrived – and cold comfortless and dreary all looks around us —— Engagements for Election prevented our being accomodated in our usual

THE LETTERS

good quarters – therefore we were obliged to content ourselves with those of a new house – one door invitingly open another repellingly closed – telling the world by a great dashing sign that it was a paradise within and preaching want of everything or of time to procure *every thing*/any thing – but *half* ready to recieve custom yet unwilling to let such a profitable load depart – they have fairly caught us – and we must get ourselves down to "Be content with what we have" "Little be it or much"

This is not the 1st neither the second nor yet the 3d time that I have written to the Boston minister — though he may have realized but one single scrawl — and while I think of it let me inform the gentleman that I have not forgotten how to love and that with the strength of my heart ——

And no wonder you thought among my many cares I should forget to send to the post office for your promised letter. But by dint of repeating it to myself as I went along or thanks to my capital memory – I remembered that I ought to send on Wednesday night ——

N.B. Remember to scold Waldo – heartily – and sincerely for a part of the second page of his epistle

I must tell you now of our plans for if I get engaged in prating of other things you may whistle for one bit of information – Here we shall tarry untill Wednesday morning when we leave for Northampton and shall not go to Middletown as we at first proposed. At

1829

Northampton we shall stay 2 days at least – and perhaps shall go from there to B—— but of this hereafter. I have seen to day 2 or 3 trees in the glory of full blossom – without one single leaf of green – and I verily believe that such a beauty in Mass cannot be found —— And these showers that descend so gloomily savour of summer much – and have tended to put the last finishing coat of richness to the velvet verdure all about us —— I look at all the beautiful things and murmer "I wish he were here" and amongst them do ungratefully think & feel a wee bit sadly – and wherefore? – simply because – this heart of mine has left loving the green trees and fields best of all on earth. It is a silly song that saith We meet on earth to part no more – but that that tells of a meeting in the Land o' the Leal – is one of the songs of comfort to me —— It drives away all the evil spirits and absent or present from my earthly friend, is an equally valuable hope to me –

I paint you often in your study – often in your daily walks – *sometimes* opening the red morroco case – as for me I do not love to look at your miniature — 'tis so speechless and says any thing in the world but – "Nelly I love you" though were it to utter these words I would not hesitate to say promptly and from my soul No —— "Ellen I regret you" would be fitter much and suit the forboding expression —— Who would delight in the motionless ivory when the moving speaking original is yet so freshly before me

– and of 2 pictures I would contemplate the best ——

I write but feebly in my journal – and but feebly now —— and all I can say or plead in excuse is that I tire of a minutes work —— *But* I grow stronger and I feel happier every day I live — Hear me oh King! — I will write you tomorrow again — God bless you! ——

The *Ladies wish* to be *remembered to* the Young Man —— I wish you would thank your Mother most heartily for her good letter to me ——

This fragment of a poem is in R.W.E.'s handwriting on a small sheet of paper, folded over and tucked into one of Ellen's notebooks.

And do I waste my time
Scribbling of love to my beautiful queen
And is it idle to talk in prose and rhyme
Of one who at midnight & morning's prime
In daylight is fancied, in visions seen?
And do I forget the burning crown
That Glory should weave of light for me –

[4]   (*Hartford May 6 1829*)
                               Hartford Tuesday —

    Oh Grandpa!! If my half grown ideas do give you pleasure in the least degree — the growth of a little spot enfeebled by disease keenly alive to every wind that blows and chilled by every cloud that o'ershadows What must the posies create in my heart which you send to me — rich full blown flowers — evergreens — such as weary the senses not a bit — and 10 years hence if I may be with you – I shall read them with as much pleasure as now — because they are not unmeaning love letters – written *only for courtship* — I surely have seen such —— It is not that I fear you will doubt my common sense when I withold papers from you – for I seldom write a word without some meaning – though I would not blame you if you found it hard to credit such an assertion – and I have often a deep meaning that for lack of Herberts *herb* for *expression* is hidden obscured almost entirely — and I seemed to have tucked a parcel of words together without awakening a single sympathetic feeling in the breast of the reader – How deplorable the case and oh how much more so if it were not Waldo that was destined to read such things – and puzzle his poor eyes to pick out the words from the scrawl and the meaning from the words —— How vastly miserable *his* task. It behooves me as I love you – to interest myself for your eyes & senses – therefore Grandpa I wont

1829

give you any papers written before this date   Hear Grandpa? ——

I wonder if your eyes will for ever remain shut to the dark spots of your Ellinelli's soul – Do you remember what I told you one day – which you pshaw'd at furiously – I assured you I was hard hearted and I told you the thermometer would rise often to an alarming height on trifling occasions – therefore if the lover persists in closing his eyes fast – let not the *husband & lover* start to find his *wify* told true stories of herself. You have seen her gentle and you loved the temper — Oh the mysterious maid   says the parson – what a depth she pretends to inhabit!!! But all this prosing came of my eyes resting on the beginning of the second page of your epistle about the domain which you choose to call beautiful – beautiful to lover's eye – It is late   I will talk to you again tomorrow – and Oh Waldo – dear Waldo – if it is an atom added to your enjoyment when you hear I love you dearly – "I say it"   I *feel* it ——

Wednesday –

Who doubts you   Grandma? *you* lessen your dignity thus? Surprising!!!!

After I bade you Goodnight I was feasted with some splendid musick – a serenade to the Gov who tarries here – at Morgans — We were delighted yesterday by the military parade —— The Gov is one of the tamest most awkward of men – his external you'll understand He seemed frightened to a shadow by the deference paid him – but to return to the musick of last night which was perfectly entrancing and it brought sweet thoughts of you with its melody — for just before the serenaders quitted their station under the windows – the full band ceased – and one of the softest flutes in the world played "Auld lang syne" s-l-o-w-l-y till there was not a single nerve within me but what danced blythely to the song —— But here it is Wednesday and we still at Hartford – did I not write my Lord the King – that we should start on this day for Northampton? —— We have been persuaded by promises of fine sights & sounds to come – to stay till tomorrow —— I wish you were here I *do* —— For though you do not love musick extravagantly yet such as I heard last night requires not a permit [from] the ear to visit the heart – but knocks at the h[eart] too loudly to be refused —— I wish you were here – but I shall see you if all continues smooth as now a week from Thursday next – from tomorrow

I feel possessed with the idea that you will write me at N—— do not – for we know not whether we tarry a day or an hour – but for fear you should not recieve this in time to avoid such a calamity I shall tell somebody to inquire for letters and send whatever they may find to Worcester – so dont fret – had I my way I'd stay at N—— a week – or till I recieved the nosegay ——

The sisters are well and still hold their friend in remembrance – The Lady mother shameth her dafters by her fleet step and merry laugh – The Ellen loses

1829

but little from the falcon feature – is well, happy –
and thine truly ——

I have recieved both of your Hartford letters – and
have seen nought of the cousins ——

[5]   (*Worcester 12 May 1829*)
                                  Worcester

"We've been roaming, we've been roaming
Where the river views are sweet
And we're coming, and we're coming
Soon shall *we* in Boston meet ——"
                            Ellinelli's song

Dear Waldo —

First in heart comes first on paper – I thank you for your letter which I have just recieved – and if I had time I should thunder 3 pages directly – taking aim-fire (as boys say) at you, or at Boston. But as this is for your eye tomorrow my story must be shortened —— Sorry am I that it happened thus – I fain would tarry on the road – till Friday – for Boston without you seems horrible truly —— We shall start for Concord probably on Tuesday ——

My heart will plague me till I speak about the part of your letter which I still read over and over — and have vainly endeavored to recall any part of mine that could have been thus misconstrued – and I sigh sometimes for the glass window with which to let you see for yourself what passes in the inner man — No! in the 1st place I've more independance than to be governed by the measure my friend deals to me – if he merits love I'm sure I care not if he gives me but a pint   I shall give him an ocean   and have confidence that as far as I merit I also shall recieve – and although you may say – if you wish to be loved   love — I say — you may not always be loved in proportion as you love —— What will you think of this dear Waldo —— Will you say that I insinuate *one* naughty thing – no! it all came into my head because I do so love you and if ever I feel like a queen it is when I am expressing that feeling – I'm proud I can boast of it as an inmate of my breast   I am proud that it was inspired by such an one —— Dont lift up your eyes and hands in amazement dire and say "Ellinelli has become distracted and spatters ink about" — but laugh heartily and rejoice with me that we meet again if God pleases next Friday ——

Your letters to Northampton are safe – I have much to say to you more than can be well said and understood (things *so deep of import*) before the Tuesday comes — and I am now trespassing on my allotted time – Mother & sisters are well – they speak afftly of you and yet they think it a wonder of wonders that I rejoice to be so near Boston —— such a pleasant journey! say they   what would she have? —— If this letter is Spanish to you   wait till I come – and love me till then trusting that I shall explain all in manner most satisfactory ——

   Thine am I ever
      Ellen
 Forgive the blots ———

1829

[6] *(Derry May 23 1829)*
Derry

Dear R. Waldo
"I have a great regard for you"   I love you dearly —

[7] *(Concord May 1829)*
Saturday night – 10 o'clock

I had planned dear Waldo to devote all the aft to you – but my body could not agree with the strong – earnest inclinations of my spirit —— The head refused to indite and the hand to be scribe – but it is not wicked to steal this half second to tell you how *very* constantly I think of you – and how firmly I am bound to you – In your vespers remember me – remember earnestly *yourself* as you love me —— I would write I will write a long long letter the very first moment when I feel as if you would be happier for what I shall say – I am so thankful for your letters that I bless you always as I read them though it be the 20th time —— Good night   dear Waldo says Ellen T ——

The things have arrived from Mrs Chandlers – and I am sorry you should have had one care about them

[8] *(Concord May 1829)*
Concord — New chamber

Dear Waldo –
I cannot persuade myself that it is only 6 days since

THE LETTERS

we parted —— Old greybeard has just begun to feel the weight of years – and takes the liberty of travelling slowly – and the privilege of depending on other than his own staff to help him along —— My Mother my bretheren my sisters are all around me but where is the new found toy? – I beg pardon. — I meant merely to discover *myself* to you – not to offend you by such an insignificant comparison – but babies cannot live without the plaything they love best — and *I* can but impatiently endure to be away from the thing I like best in the world —— Now as you're a grown up man – *you* it becometh not to fret and whine and wish – but what can be better expected from *me*?

Concord should be dear to me and in one way it *is* endeared —— and Paradise (which Mr. Thomas thinks is wrongly —/not rightly/— named) *is* Paradise – in my (*eye dear*) and you know for why — I was there at 6 this morning – and imagined I could hear the echoings of the french words yet whispered among the trees – though they were first borne on the breath of winter they proved all too warm and melted its icy coldness and now they live on the summer air and I believe they were wafted to me – I do I do —— When you come up we'll say them to each other and it will be an ever-green spot on the face of the earth ——

Waldo says "Are not the affections in our own power?" I say No! —— Every day I say – No! —— I wrote so to somebody once who was vexed that I

1829

could not *try* & love him —— And what an idea! to try and pick out all the little points that offered resistance that I might be such as he — the tall creepers of affection chose still to waver in the breeze and bear their own weight than cling to such support – and wave they did – till they rested on what was designed for them and where they never will die – they never will wither one atom ——

I like not to believe what you say about the mind —— You can hardly believe it or love to believe your friend has so little power to sketch — I'll try not to believe it as many do truths that closely fit and fret them — though if the concern were wholly mine how frightful would the painting be —— Only think that ever I should have anything beautiful in my inner man — and so utterly hidden – Alas! teach me to draw it forth if it be so — teach me to paint in strong colours —— If I learn not soon God will lose what belongs to him as the inventor and former of this soul of mine ——

If the indian towel would wipe uttered sentences away – or their memory – I'd hang a piece around my neck — I dare to say more than *every other sentence* would vanish – why then should I not use it as second thought dictates —— I wiped away in the journal a long page about Mrs Lyman — and a still longer about an acquaintance at Hartford – both of whom I knew not one bit — and had no right to be enraptured [or] displeased with either — I was justified surely in judging by what I saw at least none can help this – but nonsense guided my pen when I copied the picture —— Notwithstanding Grandpa my heart is a stranger to the tender passion – yet I do feel too much regard for you to allow you to be shocked by what I know should displease you —— there rest a minute — take a short nap – and you will read the rest better —— Your protestations – Yes! where lies the utility? — come let us agree – we will say no more of the foolish thing — perhaps the flame will die having nought to feed on — remember now you are not to say – *or feel* any warmer or kindlier feeling to *me* than to Aunt Mary — nor I than to Aunty Washburn —— Well having entered into this agreement I hope Rev R. W. E. will remember that one month from yesterday he has agreed to come to Concord N H — Mr Thomas will expect him – all his friends will anticipate his visit with happiness being quite a popular preacher and pleasing & fine in his *everyday walk* —— If Mr Breed cannot accomodate him – Mr Kent has enlarged his mansion by a late alteration and upon an emergency would not object to boarding him if his stay be short —— Mother is rather enfeebled by the sudden heat – Paulina & Margaret are very well — and all speak often and affectionately of you The new chamber they call *mine* how good they are – I did not ask but they read in my eye – I had more to be alone for than they – and as usual they gave to me what they would have delighted in themselves — I wish the world was filled with such as they — those who know them well wish with me I know

1829

—— I want to charge you never to let a letter lay in the drawer will you remember – as you think of me and believe me – let every one find its way to me as soon as they can possibly — Now Waldo do — I say nothing about the writing but when written do not delay to send ——

                                     Ellen T

2d Monday – I am hoping to hear to night from you – and I want to tell you my saddle horse is beautiful – very easy and very manageable — I ride to night with Eliz Sparhawk – who poor child is worn with woe — and reproaches from her lover & her friends —
   a mother who urges her sair
   Her father does na speak
   But looks in her face Till her heart is like to brak –

[9]   (*Concord May 1829*)

"Come gentle patience smile on" Waldo – This very hour did I recieve a letter from the King which was a bracer to Ellinelli's heart – she fretted last week because her head forbade her to write and scolded this week because she did not hear from Boston and Papa's letter said nought of the ease of the King —— I will not plague you with such puzzling scrawls so often when I get a little wonted to my lonely state of life but talk to you now I *must* & *will* and forgive the nonsense which naturally flows from my

35

THE LETTERS

brain when I do not stir it beforehand —— How funny that I should be thinking at the same time with you – of going to Paradise to find the dear words – I wept for pure gladness at the thought that we had been stirred (this word is stirred) with the same idea – But you say you recieved no word Monday Eve from me & wherefore? I sent one or two words for you and was almost ashamed to send another letter on Monday Evening for fear of the *dread Postmaster*'s laugh! or of Mr Adams wonder at 3 Concord letters one on the heels of another –

The warm weather sends us about the house like troubled spirits – and *I* yes *I* am the most erect and blooming among the tribe – and even take upon myself the sweet office of lifting up the feeble hands of my kindred – God will spare me to be useful I humbly hope and I may yet prove a staff for *somebody* —— You may say, boast not — remember the Monday in Jan. —— I do — I do — With gratitude to God with gratitude to my friends – and with a glowing heart to my *friend* do I think of last winter —— it was a blessed sickness and a blessed season that was the means of making us better acquaint – that knit our souls more firmly – that admonished me of my frailty and thanklessness ——

Wed. aft —

How it must weary you poor fellow to puzzle through these obscure labyrinths – One would imagine I had lived on Brown's Philosophy – shall I tell

1829

you what I have been doing since I left the *rich* city and became poor? for the *shadow* of my wealth is all I can certainly call my own – and that not without my hand rested this instant upon it – Well then I have read very little (but that is what I have *not* been doing) I have played much knowing that Time steps merrily to certain tunes – and I have read the King's instructive & amusing – merry yet solid letters often I have read in the Morrocco case by Miss Goodrich a great deal I have rode on the King's horse (Marmion by name) and his easy motions gave me time & chance to dream of the King most delightfully ——
I have been to the poor house where a poor wretch lies – breathing so shortly and wasting so fast – that I hope God in his mercy will take him away shortly – this is the poor Lovejoy that has ever been a cripple and I dare say you saw him – he has been but a few months sick but his sufferings are dreadful and each breath brings a world of woe — I have walked — but not to Paradise – I have written a great deal and I have sat drumming my fingers – (to my shame be it spoken) and wondering of the King's thoughts – the King's bodily feelings – does he smile? does he regret anything? Is he as happy as he might be? Oh can I make him one bit happier? Will he *tell* me if I can?
—— Mr Thomas accompanied Mary Jane to Claremont on Sat but to the great surprise of all the matchmakers on Monday he returned without the fair lady who will come day after tomorrow She is rather sad – I wish sincerely she may be prospered in

affairs both spiritual & temporal —— Mr Farmer called yesterday to see us — looks thin as usual – & a deal more languid thanks you for some book you sent him most heartily – & *he as well as Mr Thomas* trusts you will not disappoint him of the promised visit in June ——
 I have read Scougal's Life of God & I like it & wish it were more concise ——
Dear Waldo when Elizabeth Sparhawk tells me the woe she has experienced this winter – and all from an engagement formed too rashly   I shudder & then rejoice —— She said – "We were acquainted   Ellen only 2 months" —— 2 months!! we were *acquainted* Waldo only 2 weeks – and we seem so perfectly known to each other and (I will say) so perfectly satisfied with each other – if *I* made discoveries – they enrich me – and I thank God for his wonderful goodness ——
I seem to be the only one left for this poor girl to confide in she has blame and slander from all quarters – none considering the least of the evils would be to live unmarried than to tell a direct falsehood in promising to "love honour" &   I hold my breath when I think of the risk   the uncertainty of the destiny of a heart rushing impetuously as it does to link itself to its supposed companion —— The journey is hard back again ——
 I will have mercy upon you – and now you see that I have been too lazy to stir my brain for your edification and if you had rather I would not write ever again such weakness – tell me frankly – and I'll wait

1829

longer for the collection of the sensibles —— I love you – but better than the King loves Ellinelli – this is to express what is inexpressible

The bundles have reached us —— When you write to your Mother please give my love, my best love to her ——

[10] *(Concord June 1829)*
Ellinelli's chamber

You need not open your eyes wider than their wont – you need not set yourself in the easiest of postures to meet an intricate soul-stirring discussion or open the treasure house to recieve a new idea — I have nothing to say for myself this aft – but that I am miserably stupid and nonsensical and were it not that I know the King ought to know me in all my character & disposition I would be mum for years before I'd devote an hour of a day like this to him – and for one other reason, that I can still tell him of the existence of the ever burning light – whose flame rises constantly steadily undisturbed by any gust of passion or stupifying mist that crosses its path ——

Tis not so much that I fear you will weary of 3 pages of mine in reading it – because it would be no great task for a *man* – or the King to read the same quantity in the spelling book or primer – but I dont like to have *all* the advantage of a correspondence on

THE LETTERS

my side and be reaping good baskets full from my friends fields and pretend to send him the same — which prove to be but husks and trash —— I'd rather begin every letter by stating the welfare of the cherished light – and then copy some useful page from some useful book for your edifi —— I say yea to the belief that the more we *know* each other the more we shall love each other – but not the more *I* talk of *myself* the more will you love me – for I have not the *developing* faculty – I cannot call out the little inhabitants and clothe them so that they may represent aught that I wish to convey — those that have the good spirits and have the good knack of making them visible as they are in all their original purity – are blest – and the more they talk of *I* the higher the *I* stands in the listeners estimation — I believe most obstinately Oh King that when God's image stampt upon my soul is shining free from the mists of sin – that my outer man will bear some of its purity and a high hope will be visible in my countenance and conduct   But the time hath not arrived and the picture is often deadened and obscured —— Nevertheless – I think its bright moments grow more frequent and more truly blessed than they used to be —— And Oh King when I see you every day – with such a firm upright bearing of soul to contemplate I shall no doubt glorify my Father more constantly which is in Heaven   Communion with him is a rare medicine for the diseases which keep us so low in our desires and hopes – I may not say communion but

1829

supplication – because communion – I understand means *converse* and God holds it not with the soul abounding in low desires ——

Last evening was to have been yours dear Waldo but the *happeners* in must have some musick and were so entirely engrossed by their psalm-singing that 10 o'clock found them in anticipation of half a dozen tunes – alas!! alas for Waldo!! thought I – but if bolts and bars can prevail tomorrow shall be his – and a gloomy day the tomorrow of yesterday proves — a little sun a little rain a cauld wind to chill the soul and pinch the body though I dinna ken frae what quarter it blaweth —— Dadd has arrived safely and most cheerily —— For more reasons than one I was delighted to see him – and for more reasons than one I asked him how our friends all were in the city – but slowly he ate and drank and slowly put his hand into his pocket and *coldly* and *slowly* handed me a packet but swiftly I sped to my chamber and left him wondering —— I enjoyed the holiday of souls twice as well for my Sat nights solace ——

Your visit in plain words – is neither an interruption to any *plan* nor aught but a beautiful green spot a redeeming spot – in the monotonous Concord life – and the sisters rejoice at the prospect and the mother lives in her daughters and blessed be she forever You're late in negotiating an exchange with our Parson or believe me to be so — no! I was afraid of disappointment so, the first time I saw Mr T—— he signified to me that he would agree to terms pro-

THE LETTERS

posed at the risque * (*Grandma forgets to modernize herself – risk) of disappointing somebody – I almost forget who – Mr Parker of Portsmouth   I believe whom he had partly promised to preach for – I thought if he could settle it with the whisperer within it was all beautiful —— I wont say *any more* to him about it – because he looks at me so archly and enquires for Boston friends – and he shall not think me so over & unbecomingly anxious – Shall he? he is a calm looker-on & professes to be heart free —— Therefore Grandpa if you will write him it will be better
  The tempest I have enjoyed – though the tempest you speak of I *believe* I have never read ——

Yea   Waldo   Yea — a torch it is – and its light hath helped me to discover many beautiful things not in the inward house though —— I recieved the treasure upon the word *Ellen* and I return you upon the word *Waldo* one of affection and truth – and [do] yet remember you night and day and please God we may live to meet again in this world and hold sweet converse ——

Mr Farmer has loaned *Mr Harvey* Courser "The Complete Angler" which the little man professes to find as interesting as Pollock's *Course of Time* and as a great favour brought it to me to read —— Father I believe has settled all matters at Mrs Chandlers trouble not thyself therefore – for thou hast already borne more than thy share — I love you Waldo dearly — I'd *write this to Aunt Washburn* herself –

1829

I was desired to desire you to bring with you the first edition of the "Morocco case" by Miss Goodrich —— I'm going to see some Indians who have taken up their abode on the banks of our river and are said to be suffering under sickness & want —— to night

[11] (*Concord 2 June 1829*)
Concord   June 2d
Grandma

My dear Waldo –
Tis late yet the will saith not "to bed" but rather wake and converse – love & rejoice – The food hath been recieved – and greedily swallowed – it maketh me strong yet is my soul so very very sad that mine eye runneth over with water ——

A sober thing this love — and the more we enjoy it – the more its dread un*certainty* presses upon us – upon *me* I should have said —— Now have patience and let my puny thoughts come as they will – and do correct the English exercise as you did the French ——
June 3d   Oh what glorious sunsets we have   I recollect when I was a *very* little girl that I never was so much angered or disturbed by anything that a dawn of glory or an eve of beauty like unto this could not insensibly calm the tumult – and make me love every body better than myself – and wonder I could ever have pouted in a world so lovely —— This was in *reality* selfish – I wrote at Londonderry a peice of compo about the beauties of sunset & sunrise which

43

THE LETTERS

the Lady Grant assured me was wonderful for a wee dumb thing – promising so little —— And she looked hard at me and questioned me whether I *really* picked the materials from my own rag-bag — but I swelled so indignantly at the supposition of a doubt that she *dreaded the consequences* — and could only wonder ever after that such a little spitfire thing should chose a subject so harmonious and lovely for a theme

10 o'clock? yes, nearly 11 – and I love you for a certainty, dearly, and I shall sleep beautifully upon the pillow of your comforting assurances   Good night —— Nightcap on and I wont gang to rest yet – but write some more

Am I not engaged? Did I not write "dear Mother" to Waldo's mother? never questioning the propriety of the thing   Though from the innocence of my heart's anticipations I said it and all things considered repent it not —— While I remember (beautiful perspicuity) I want to write to your mother – if I put a letter in the office here will she recieve it? you need not fash yourself to answer that query because Daddy can answer it —— I'm sorry   very sorry   that Edward is thin – and I wish he would come to Concord again —— Why will he not with you? I will pray for him as *Waldo's brother* and *my* friend – How do I know how much I am indebted to *his* prayers for my present well-being? —— And Charles I asked to come but he seemed to think it impossible – I made another *purple* guard for him for *I* did not like the blue — and forgot to give it him ——

1829

I dont call Scougal morose – but I mean what he thinks loses some of its weight by repetition in different words —— Mighty truths I *should* love & value now and not wait for the gray hair which perhaps will never see the head of frizzles – or the hollow cheek which I guess will not be brought by age — and thinking thus I'll read it again by & by   I've read Irving's Columbus – and the Conquest of Granada I am reading —— I'm my own mistress and will eat jellies if I like —— Rather dry pages of Dame Natures book lie open here for my perusal – but *every* page hath beauty and I love the study well —— Marmion has been very naughty and I have not been on his back for 5 days   Margaret rode him and he almost succeeded in throwing her – but we have deprived him of oats and exact his daily labour from him which I doubt not will have the good effect to sober him that I may ride him soon again ——

My walks are few – When will the time in the "month of roses" arrive? —— You are chosen Chaplain of the Senate – will it prove a preventative? – or no? Mr Thomas came last evening —— It requires not a bit of penetration I think to discover the state of his little heart – I like him much on many accounts – and I hope if he loves Mary Jane – he will not be disappointed in her —— His sermons on Sunday last were both good – and his expository lectures interesting —— What I was going to say is – That the good man offered me consolation   The session he said would be short and he doubted not but Mr E would be able to come provided he were to accept — moreover he might obtain leave of absence —— The Mother is well and happy and thanks you for your remembrances and always with the sisters desires me to tell Waldo how much (in quality/in quantity) they think of him – but I am apt to forget such sort of things – not that I do not think them *sincere* but they are always or may be always inferred "We are 5!!" —— And do remember that I always want *my* love and respects given to the *"Old Concord"* mother But [you] will not I know require of me every time I write a se[ntence] to that effect — I think they carry no meaning to the eye after a while – (the meaning goes to the eye first) and you see them at the bottom of a letter as words of course – But yet when you write such things the mother and sisters look delighted when I tell them – and often ask me whether I return any kind words to Waldo – they scold me when I say I forget it ——

The rain is coming on and the darkness of midnight and I shant write any more – perhaps *little* Hamilton Hutchins will call tomorrow early for this therefore I shall seal it to night I want to write to Aunt W and I think I shall enclose this to her ladyship —— Good night ——

(I am yours entirely now and shall be ever
Ellen L. Tucker)

Dont I write more and more slovenly – remember your promise to tell me when you wearied of these my shocking deformed scrawls ——

This poem occurs in one of R.W.E.'s notebooks of poetry, and must have been written early this summer.

I need not hide beneath my vest
Thy picture, the pride of art,
For I bear it within my breast
And the chain is round my heart.

Thine eyes still shined for me, though far
I lonely roved the land or sea;
As I behold yon evening star,
Which yet beholds not me.

With thy high form my sleep is filled,
Thy blazing eye greets me at morn,
Thou dost these days with beauty gild
Which else were trivial and forlorn.

What arts are thine, dear maiden,
O tell me what arts are thine,
To teach thy name to the rippling wave,
And to the singing pine?

This morn I climbed the misty hill
And roamed the pastures through;
How danced thy form before my path
Amidst the deep-eyed dew!

When the redbird spread his sable wing,
And showed his side of flame;
When the rosebud ripened to the rose,
In both I read thy name.

Why should I sing of thee?
The morning sings of thee;
Why should I seek thy face?
No face but thine I see.

1829

[12]   (*Concord June 1829*)

   I laughed a bit when I read your letter to think how you'd join with me in condemnations if you could know the *how* & *when* I often write you letters — the last letter you recieved (I believe) was written after every body had been abed long – yes   her Ladyship herself had tossed on her pillow nearly an hour – when thinking of something she wanted to say to the King she glided out of bed and spectre like wrapped a white garment around her – and spent 10 minutes writing to the King — I would not have presented to your imagi such a ghastly picture but for your fears – and *kind cautions* —— I should really be grieved if I *laboured* for what I write to you —— I often make the apologies because I am apt to be so dreadfully careless – and if I wrote as well (I mean in choice of language not in depth) as I would – you ken these apologies wad be deceitful and wicked —— Dear Grandpa what can you mean, by saying that harmony of language and precision and such sort of things are none of my concern — hey day!! and am not I preparing to write sermons? – and books too for *grown* people – to the edification or improvement of children I aspire not —— Yes!! I shall contend for my rights bravely though I'm but 17! There now I've got an apron to make and I leave you to your own reflections ——
   I tell u what I saw in a book just now – what you

THE LETTERS

have often said and I have thought and assented to as often —
  Be fair or foul   be rain or shine
  The joys I have possessed *in spite of fate* are mine
            (meagre consolation this. ——)

Sunday Eve —— I'm not sick but *well* — and the raven or crow or whasoever I trust has not croaked ominously   I am fleet of foot – and have left all the aches & pains far in the rear – no thanks to Marmion's "light fantastic horse shoe" – I shall ride however tomorrow morn – with daddy —— Elizabeth Sparhawk will ride with me each day hereafter — I used to think that bleeding from the heart was something more fatal than bleeding from the lungs but of late years I find more instances of complete recovery from the one than the other – though Elizabeth shews no symptoms of an abatement of her disorder —— She went with me (*a fib*) to see the Indians — and we found them very much better in situation than we thought – they have no pure language – but would catch a meaning from French sentences —— They are what I dont like and more beastly and degraded than I imagined Indians & *Canadaian* Indians could be —— They sell *all* for one drop of *"comfort"* – ardent —— Margaret has a room closely curtained so that Concord sounds sights and breezes knock in vain for admittance – here she sits all day long – but I have never applied my eye to the key hole to see what are her occupations   I'll go if you'll wait a minute – &

1829

faithfully report – I dont see her – but from the strange mutterings which reached my ear I fancy she holds conference with some invisible —— Paulina *thin as air* (expressive), goes singing from one room to another – in search of some article that has not blest our eyes for 7 or 8 years – and prying with her long nose into every corner – much to the annoyance of the methodical inhabitants of the house ——

Mary Jane has returned from Claremont — and is the most kind and affectionate of all the household ——

Oh   I am tired of talking about these things when I've got something thats leaping every moment to be said — you know the thought – the feeling – I cannot tell you – but 'tis so maddening to me that I cant pull some of the strong yearnings forth and pin them to paper – the words we are wont to write – are meek, inadequate representatives – but still I'll write them (I love you dearly, Waldo) there — dont they look like half expressed cold sort of words? Oh explain!! explain!! why for a whole year past I've been *troubled* with these deep sort of feelings – and for *6 months* past have laboured to bring them to light and do so utterly fail — I am not sad to tell you the fact but am restless because the quality and the quantity cannot be made known to you —— Silly girl! its q[uality] God knows only – that its *quantity* is immeasurable is all [I] can say ——

My window that looks into the garden is very pleasant – I am sorry to believe that the moon will be

THE LETTERS

gone before you come for the charm is by moonlight – It was a feast last night to watch the young leaves trembling and whispering under the bright rays (soft kisses) of the pale Lady — though she does not yet reveal herself wholly —— But when you come I shall forget all about moons stars leaves all but the presence of my best friend who will *be mine* eternally (presumptuous) – and dwell with me where we need them not —— Mr. Lathrop is married and so by this time is our good Mr Bouton —— Let Waldo & Ellinelli set these impatient ones a good example – and wait the bidding of Dame Nature and her interpreter Betty Jackson (Forgive)

 Dear Sir – this is Monday day — you *must recieve this Tuesday* —— yrs respectfully
Ellen Louisa Tucker ——

[13]   (*Concord June 1829*)
Dear Waldo
 For various reasons I shall write only a line or two to night — and I wish I could aid you in your *driving* affairs but wishing's vain ——
 Marmion has grown good and I have began again to revel in the exhilirating breezes produced by a *canter* mounted on his back so broad and soft I leave Concord scandal far behind and for Concord sand I care not a jot —— I can sympathize with you in your newly discovered dignity too for the white

Dear H. Waldo   Lucy

    I have a great regard for you & I love you
dearly —
    Rec'd May 23, 1829

Good bye I cannot ask you to read this dog day scrawls any more — I hope you will give me my part in the vesper service — and though last in order we found it impossible to make our vespers the same and thine together — yet we will be constant at our own hour, and constant in our hearty remembrances of each other — God bless you saith Ellen or prays it your own Ellen L. L. I should say —

haired urchins clap their hands at me as I vanish in the clouds of dust and the toads and frogs extend their leapers at the sound of Marmion's footsteps the air too is put in motion by the winnowing of the wings of affrighted redbreasts wrens et cetera Now you may bustle there in the city as you please and pride yourself upon the homage of the fickle heart of man – I am content with the deference paid me by the toads & frogs the birds and dogs whose hearts are beautifully transparent – Oh Ellinelli what a prater!!! ——

Oh Waldo do not cruelly disappoint Mr Thomas – come if it lies in your will —— Your letter he has recieved and I do hope he will be resigned if fate orders him a disappointment —— And now Friend Waldo – am I not engaged to you? yea verily – by heart & hand

    Thine truly
    Ellen T ——

Tis freedom to write to you because I do not fear a too warm conclusion How strange!! that often the flow of affectionate feeling gives offence – and is criticised as *improper* — from such a temper oh defend me

[14]   (*Concord June 1829*)
Dear Waldo —
I've got money enough more – be[cause I sent] you but $20, because I happen [to have had]

THE LETTERS

loud calls for the remainder – The little [bag] in one corner of my wallet was never drawn forth with such gleeful fingers – and lightsome heart – and I feel myself grateful, thankful, to you dear Waldo for giving me the opportunity to assist in so good a cause —— But you are coming to see me soon – my heart leaps to think o't and I'll tell you how happy you've made and are always making me —— I am fearful if I stop to say much to you my Mercury will have fled —— I ride every morning with Geo Kent who is kind and attentive to me. With Eliz Sparhawk I would ride more willingly but Mother says she cannot trust me without a squire — I shall have one soon and I love him dearly ——

After all your injunctions I did [not] neglect my last date – this is Sat [morn-]ing —— Haste thee Waldo Haste [thee] quickly to your own Ellinelli ——

Waldo did not disappoint Mr. Thomas and Ellen. According to his Preaching Record, he preached in Concord, New Hampshire, on June 21st and 28th and he stayed with the Kents. Ellen was taken sick during his visit and he had to leave on June 29th before she recovered. The first part of the following letter is written in ink by Paulina, the rest by Ellen, in pencil; her writing is quite faint and badly blurred.

[15] *(Concord, July, 1829)*
Friday 3d

Dear Waldo

To day the heavens smile again & smiling, have a pleasing effect on the Queen invalid. the weather, as

1829

you probably ken, has been such that we could not expect to see her make wonderful progress, nor yet has it retarded her progress as much as we fear'd it might for she has every day since you left trudged as far as your room as if she there expected to see your *ghost-ship* or some relic of your departed self. She has beside another inducement to extend her walk thus far her *forte, music,* being there. Nursey says "Lady tell the minister Miss Ellen since my arrival has not had a more quiet peaceful night than the last her sleep was perfectly natural without the least appearance of the distress we have frequently observed since your departure; she says too, tell him; 'tho Miss Ellen never told me she regretted your absence yet do you think I did not see it in her tell tale eyes yes even without my *spectacles*: Dear Waldo you do not know how grateful I feel for the novel it came in very appropos for we have sent to the library's here but it was not obtainable & and the ear of the Lady E is weary of hearing the contents of the few books our little library contains. The Queen's poney, I know you feel a slight degree of interest in him, therefore I will report to you his proceedings & how he carry's himself since his Master left us my neck is not seriously injured tis to be hoped, but — guess why O because I have not been on his back once but he has been rode & we are thinking how much he again stands in need of the parsons good counsel; In our good parson Sudwitz too I cannot but believe you feel an interest need I assure you he is no longer a

THE LETTERS

prisoner of *Hope* nor yet of *Dispair* yet who will deny that he is a prisoner of some sort or kind he is surely made captive & confined by *silken* bands at least; his captivity commenced the 1st day of July 1829 & yet independance is nigh at hand very well tis a joyful occasion & tomorrow in all probability we shall hear the roar of the mighty canon: Dear W should there be the slightest change in E for the worse rest assured you shall hear of it quick as the fleetest horses can be procured to carry the inteligence & you shall also be able to mark tho you can not be eye witness, the rapid advancement she makes towards health To day we threatened to give her a ride but with us the — wind as you may suppose has not blown kindly being East due, blue East: Cousin Susan T is with us which maketh the footsteps of old Time pass less perceptably which maketh the ♡ of the damsel more joyous, less sad. with love more than this will contain from Parents Sisters & Cousins I remain your truly affec.
 Sist. Poll

Dear Friend –
 I cannot stop to peruse the above yet I know it must be correct and of course satisfactory to your *honour* — remember I'm calm as a clock and I do *not think it presumption* to address you as my *dear friend*.
 "Love *flows like the Solway but ebbs like its tide*" and oh how much more conducive to my health is this cool substantial indifference that I have so (un)-

1829

successfully courted — now you may tell all believers in the ardent temperament and its injurious tendencies what a miraculous change hath befallen me — and more than ever will the Bermuda plan be approved – its warm breezes will be more than ever grateful ——

Waldo the parting prayer murmered over my pillow is sweetly recieving its answer — God is with me and I feel he is making me well — and I am determined myself to write you every day for the worry lest they should fail will hurt me much more as [I have] at last convinced all and I write a thousand letters to you [daily] in my head which are only interrupted by Nursey's saying Wa'nt it funny Miss Ellen? an enquiry respecting some yard long story or other which she might as well tell to the rocking chair or Old Morpheus himself —— Her voice hath become to mine ear like a very pleasant rain — it but lulls to sweet thoughts and off to darling dreams – giving me merely the satisfactory assurance of companionship —— I recieved a good letter from Mrs Lyman last night wherein she begs of Waldo Emerson to inform her aught he may chance to know of a Mr Green preaching at Cincinnati — character et cet. Now dear Waldo when you think of me think I am getting well – am cheerful, happy, – grateful and yours entirely and will we not both be happy? We have heaven and earth before us in which to live and love each other and though we find not [where] to lay our [heads] we will not fail of rest and a "harvest time of love" in heaven —— The air will be sweeter there the more our senses may have endured of earth's pestilence   say you not so? — Be a good boy — let our paths if decreed be miles apart here we meet and taste heavens joy together my [*blurred*] ——

My parents dear and sisters dear are well and do speak very affectionately of you ——

I wish I could see that [*illegible*] come again, remember me to her and tell her I would [*illegible*] — and to Charles and Edward I hope you will speak for me —— Naughty that I had said nothing about them when you went [away] but when people know me they do not expect it —— I always mean all I say about respects etc. regards etc but I seldom say [half] I mean ——

The pills arrived.

[16] *(Concord   July 1829)*

Papa will come down next week – and I think Mother when he returns will take a trip to the city —— I wish I could go too but – but – but — ah!! ——

[17] *(Concord July (?) 1829)*
Sunday

I have had beautiful hours to day   my dear friend my ministering angel of a cousin has read and soothed

1829

me with sermon and sweet psalm and now the day is departing and the "hymn of life" does shed over me its comforting influences — O thou consoler – But I am absolutely out of my senses you will think and I wont frighten you at the *beginning* of such an overwhelming length of epistle —— I recieved your letter last night and I hope one from sister P did reach you —— What was written therein so favorable – continues still true only I guess the Ellinelli may boast a firmer gait from chamber to chamber and a wee bit keener palate She thinks of you though seldom speaking of you and cries shame to herself for counting so oft the hours days & minutes since you bade adieu She pants to get her feet out of flannel and away from hot bottles – and nurses kind though annoying arm binding her like the supporting hoop of a weak butter tub – she would fain fling away —— Ungrateful girl – there's not one thing that she reasonably desires she hath not

The beauties of the season which she cannot gather for her own enjoyment – are brought in profusion by the good friends and never was captive prince or queen so well attended or *strictly guarded*. The rest of the acts of Ellinelli are they not written in the memories of past days? —— How could you tempt me thus? —— Here you say in the end of your letter – if I should be better any time to see you why you'll come – now this is really naughty of you – why I read it with such longings to see you and then so conscious that it will be of no benefit at least none to

THE LETTERS

be considered in such circumstances — we shall meet I hope in health and happiness soon —

Dr Jackson can be coaxed out of his determinations I was going to say – but you didn't try to do so and "the business is" that the plan more than ever displeases me owing to some fresh objections which in pulling the matter to pieces I have raised   These again it belongs to Betty Jackson to remove – but Mother *must* see him – you are an *awkward* person (excuse me) to employ in such matters   not but what you have most gracefully, satisfactorily and wonderfully transacted business thus far for which you have recieved the loud praises of my mother to say nothing of certain little inexpressibles glowing in Ellinelli's bosom – but I am determined it is the last thing you shall undertake in such a delicate sort of an affair   So there   this between you and I

Better Aunt Mary should see me now with unruffled night cap and quaker fashioned hair – than with the India wrought comb and full sleeve of the time ——

In my opinion the more in the prevailing ton you deck yourself the easier you glide along – little sleeves and 3 inch bonnet rims would be death to the wearer now and it requires less thought and attention to dress in Turkey like *the Turkies* than a studied plainness and eccentricity —— To say nothing of the superior attraction of a yard wide bonnet rim — " 'tis distance lends enchantment to the view" ——

Cousin Susan is lovely as mortal may be and com-

1829

forts me exceedingly —— Mother thanks you for your letter to her – Father is very kind to me – Mary Jane is good – Sisters Peg and Poll need no praise of mine – Rosanna will not sleep but guards me every night with watchful eye – Sally twists gracefully upstairs every day to kiss my hand – Eliza is constantly my first visitor every morning – and Harvey rejoices as much as I do every time he brings a letter for me – *which must always be* from Mr Emerson
Dear Waldo I love you says Ellen T ——

Will you ask Betty Jackson if Philadelphia air for winter would not be delightful & healthy ——

[18] (*Concord   July 1829*)
Dear Waldo

I am well almost and have rode 1 half of a mile this day am greatly refreshed by it and tomorrow if the sun will only shine I'll ride again   and a'nt you glad? — I hope I shall hear from you to night – how very unreasonable – to desire of you so much – but I live on hope now a days and contrary to the usual effect which such diet hath on men – I grow ruddy and hearty – "I *waste* not" & I say with deep gratitude I "want not" — My hopes are very numerous and their colours are constant ——

I wish I knew what you are doing every moment whether you pine under my proffessions of stoical indifference or whether your eagle eye   more ac-

THE LETTERS

customed to penetrate the thin veil and the thick of human depravity doth see the rosy god pretending to sleep and winking when you look and smiling in spite of himself —— You know tyranical monster that you are or you presumtously believe that a few warm words from you will cause him to spring and shake his "purple wings" But allow me to doubt your power – and to believe that my commands will more readily be complied with ——

Friend Emerson — that I want to see thee much I will confess but that thy power over me is so great as as as I'm clane run out forgive forgive

Afternoon of Monday ——
Dont you remember promising me that St Augustine poem —— Oh if your eye chance to light upon it fail not to send it me to read —— And why may not I tease you for papers and English exercises? – You that have rolls innumerable of such — Oh do send me some to read ——

Anne of Geierstein — I like pretty well this far – I mean it interests me – I must read it *all* to judge of the worth She is a misty maiden yet but I hope as the tale proceeds the clear sun will break through and make all intelligible I should like to have the fairy in me I think – I guess I should be sure to beat then when I went on my stealthy errand on St Vals day – I will as it is —— Oh what a dream was mine on Sat night I'd love to have it come to pass – and if I read my dear friends heart aright so would he ——

1829

I hope you will give my love to *our* mother when you write —— Good bye   I have written now a page & a half more than my limits allow — and yet have I said what I have been prompted to 50 times? No! not I ——

I am your own Ellen T ——

Do not be alarmed lest my senses have flown

[19]   *(Concord, 8 July, 1829)*
Wednesday aft —

I shall write you but a word or two to day though I am weel as usual – Papa will *embark* for Boston tomorrow – if his pockets afforded good accomodations for invalids he would not go alone but nursey seems indispensible at present and as to burthening the poor man so 'tis wicked to name it —— I blame myself much for not always acknowledging your thoughts as I recieve them   but oh how careless   how careless I am and thereby do I pain my dear friends and cause myself many tears by so many works *meet for repentance* ——

Let me see – 4 letters I have recieved and is it all? – if I have lost *one* I shall not get well so quick by one omission of sovereign balm — abruptly but with love in my heart toward you I must bid farewell – burn burn this   do   as you value my character as a rational being —

Ellen T ——

THE LETTERS

I shall send this by mail as Dadd goes not
I have taken a mile long ride this aft   and am   or shall be tomorrow no doubt   vastly better for it —— Mine eye is restless and mine ear tireth of sounds —— Mine arm will not entwine willingly with any — nor my foot keep step with any —— My thoughts are not with me at all   at all —— They think me very sleepy – "all owing to weakness"   and in truth I have not slept while day lasted this great while —— Cousin Susan says – or I read on waking, in her speaking eye "how dull and uninteresting are engaged cousins" I am become an island surrounded by a sea of thoughts — oh egotism what a pompous display of my great self ——

The white lilly has blown and it hath caused me to read often and to admire the pretty little peice   how do you spell (piece) in Sab Recreations   Yes the silver vest she hath put on and burst the silken sheaf or I guess she burst the sheaf first – I dont like it half as well as the snow drop though —— It hath been roughly used by the Concord gales – for they plucked it for me to day and the leaves were every one of them soiled with dirt — owing to the winds presuming to kiss the damsel with unclean face. Hold your head high as you may – disdain even to glance at the despicable – yet will they find some way to stain to *the eye* the beautiful white of the garb – but like the innocent the lilly disdaineth to flinch or close her petals against the annoyer – conscious that her purity remaineth and trusting in Heaven – patiently waiting

1829

its own time for the breeze that will blow the light stain away and she shall dazzle men with her undiminished and unrivaled loveliness booh!! booh!! what a figuration and how finished – even like "the hydra" that one of the members of court last week (3 weeks ago) insisted should "*be drawn up by the roots*! and its *fangs exterminated*" as well do I chatter and understand Rhetorick as this same member —— let me assure you I am rational though filled with unconnected thoughts — but a feeling still pervades my *whole* self – and ever shall —— I do most ardently and sincerely —— desire to be remembered to all friends
E T ——

[20] *(Concord July 1829)*
Dear Waldo

I have not forgotten you for I wrote a long long letter to you yesterday which was filled with thoughts so black and images so dire that I committed the foul thing to the winds which refused to bear it away from my sight even and it now lies a monument of my real *ugliness* beneath my window —— It is selfish to vent our black moods on our friends our *nearest* and *dearest* too – and to day I ask myself with astonishment why I even allow such to come over me – I have every thing to assist me in combat with them – and who that have in good earnest declared war against these invaders and gave their souls to the fight but came off conquerors — say — King — Are you troubled with these wretches? You will answer Nay – no doubt & say you have never a moment to spare to undo the door and let them in – Well – the Queen looks forward with delight to the time when whatsoever her hand findeth to do she shall do with all her might – she can love with her might now — Love is a treacherous door keeper he opens to friend and foe ——

Margaret   Paulina & cousin Susan have gone to the Shaker Village to day – I miss them much and hope they may not be invited by the beauty of the scene or the promise of *peace* which it speaks to tarry with them —— It would seem if "there's peace to be found in the world" "the heart that was humble might hope for it *there"* — such a sabbath day feeling it gives one — But the impression that is so beautiful, made at first sight – is I believe never strengthened by acquaintance with the Brothers and sisters of the quiet land — Angels I'm sure dont wear Shaker bonnets or hats ——

Sisters are neither of them very robust and they think of journeying with Pa as soon as the visit to the city is accomplished — The White Hills they talk about a good deal — but *I* guess not —

Eliza Mellen writes me of shaking hands with you Mrs Lobdell also cheers me by a flourishing account of the King's health & spirits – Why Grandpa you're growing young again! — and here am I fading away and passing you on my journey far – and now to think you've tired of me   and instead of trying to o'er take

1829

me you've gone back   and hope to retrace your steps quietly I suppose   till you come to the sweet sunny places of childhood – Grandpa you may go back and you may find the spots again and your cheek may be springing with richness and your eye bright with health but your spirit knows too much – that cannot be free as in days past – You have seen so many bright suns clouded and so many green spots withering that your soul will be filled with distrust – Let me warn you – you'd better not depend on quitting my company —— Waldo   have I told you lately any thing about the state of my heart? — with regard to its glowing affecs   No! well then – I am inclined to believe from certain commotions in this restless organ at certain sounds and certain thoughts that amongst other complaints with which I am afflicted and which entitles me to the most fragile corner on the list of invalids — I have certainly contracted the disease of Love —— People seem to think it is not dangerous – and say all has been done that is possible   but I think it is a very dreadful thing and I should wish my friends would have more charity for me and when I suffer so much not treat me – like a dyspeptick – Please tell me if you know aught of this complaint – and believe me there is one who can sympathize sincerely with your woes — bah   what am I doing? – what a scrawl is here – and I have not told you yet that we have hunted every crack and corner that we can think of yet – for the pamphlet but wait a giff and we will find it I guess ——

  The day comes languidly on and I'm going to dream

of you a moment — I hope you will not pout at such a whip syllabub sort of a letter – I wish I could see you now —— Goodbye Friday – aft

Dont expect Mother too confidently it is as uncertain as the wind her visit to B—— dependant all on this fickle body of mine.

[21] (*Concord July 1829*)

Oh the pleasing variety of nurses countenance – O the pleasing variety of bottles & pillows Oh the pleasing variety of toasted cracker & cream —— What say you my dear Waldo? would you not like again to be here — here — where the beautiful hours lagg not despite *they are burthened* with *deep reflection* and *noble deeds* — here where the scene tries not – where sources of refreshment and vigorous exercise for mind & body lie invitingly open – The sheperd boy relished not the soft nothingness of the castle of Indolence – and he pined for his sweet labours giving zest to his allotted hours for repose — and making his bread of coarsest brown taste richer by far than the princely fare (pound cake & the like) of the Castle —— He has returned to his ninety and nine – but – ah – there is one that he must soon return and seek diligently till he find – Waldo don't you laugh *now* – I *am* more like a sheep than any thing just at present – and if I only had a bell around my neck it would be perfect – for I wink my eyes just like one – and my long face all longings for any thing better than itself — this is the character of a great piece of beautiful musick though I own sometimes the soul by the sentiment ~~so stirring~~ ~~a ———~~ of the ~~soul~~ and a tune well adapted may be excited to nobler hopes & wishes — And it is (strange as it may appear) more apt to have this effect upon ~~a performer~~ an auditor than a performer. Where are the verses that were the effect of your two favorite tunes — were they not ruined and why were they not copied immediately under your confession of their existence — Did you give them to the fair ~~nymphs~~ who entertained you so much to your liking? Or did you send them to be published in Willis's periodical? There how cutting!!! —

Shall I send you this letter? No — yes — yes I will with its scratches which trouble me not they disfigure the letter but that they do take up your precious time sadly to steer between them and glean one whole connected, sensible thought in the whole —
I have many interruptions ——— and not unfrequent a severe scolding in the midst of one of my most sentimental effusions —
If you do not come for a week or a gain you are too good & just to believe that the quee~~n~~ has ceased to love and confide in you — or to think that your face would be a stranger to her — Let not such ugly thoughts ever darken your brain ——— Mother will write you I think — I love you faithfully and eternally —
Ellen T

Dear Waldo,
    You have had a golden day for your departure and the sun is smiling its last most sweetly at this moment — the memory of our beautiful last acquaintance filleth me, so that I scarce believe you are gone — the Last man, the Rainbow, Byron's best to say nothing of certain tightness to my ear fuller, richer, weightier, but than either I cherish most fondly for they i[s] live within me yet —. Your books have feasted me too this day truly Waldo Emerson they delight me — place not a barrier between us, or think that the deepest you write is altogether incomprehens to me — It will be useful to me such as there — give me more I pray of you — As to papers you will be poorly paid for I can find but here & there a stray bit for you — but you ken we are to live together and I will see if I cant write some more one of the lazy days in winter — and I do dearly love you — you better & better and the words grow more & more expressive & solemn — God bless you Waldo

1829

and my Moses like appearance & nursey following always behind me like the driver – ha! I laugh when I'm alone to think o't —

When I think of you now it is as somebody that has been going from me every hour every letter I recieve, the idea is conveyed, that you are much farther from me than when you wrote the last – Well be it so – go along – as fast as you can   always steering toward the same and by & by you'll come pat on Old Concord again – Old Concord forsooth – you may find Mr & Mrs Thomas there but a long Tucker nose you will not have the happiness to see — they are fools no longer   to turn blue & grey & green 'neath a winter sky – where noses form so prominent a part of the frame as in us they should be our thermometers and be duly consulted —— We take our turns at toiling at the pillars which support our household – yesterday for an hour we united our efforts and accomplished much —— Yes and *I*   poor feeble I was not the least among those who were influential in shaking the building   I address Ma with the song Come o'er the sea by Thomas Moore — She replies by singing Ne'er o'er the sea by Philip Carragan —— *This looks like success* ——

Yes – Mr Thomas is engaged at last — the fire of restless excitement is quenched – and we look for cool, calm, blessed days   I sincerely wish *them* many such – I would chuse for a wedding present to give them a bottle of the water of Oblivion — No! am I naughty? No! I am not in so saying ——

THE LETTERS

I went to ride this morn and I am going this aft again – when I come home I'll tell you all about it ——Well dear Waldo I've been breathing the beautiful air and I am most astonishingly refreshed and I want to tell you that I love you very much and I would like to have you love me always if consistent with your future plans ——

My lady Mother will come to Boston somtime ere the week expires probably – say Friday – but it is all uncertain she is well – and the sisters are pretty well and very good – and Cousin *Sowsan* is with us yet – and many a Concord beau withers & blooms neath her frown or smile – and many a humbly expressed invitation have these *"pris'ners of hope"* speered at the persecuted damsel for her sweet company in a romantic ride – a shaker party a raspberry frolic & the like but cruelly she cries "bad is the best" and they can only look and admire in silence and despair ——

The Concordians are all kind to me and I am grateful they all send somcthing to please some a little love some a little fruit and some their sweetest buds – one of these you should have seen a darling thing it is and its name is Ellen Tucker Virgin – a very fairskinned blue eyed babe with a tinted cheek like a pink shell – or as it say in "My early days" as if the cunning hand of nature had inserted rose leaves under its transparent skin —— Eliz Sparhawk is gone to Portsmouth and the family will move there in Oct —— I wish you knew her better – I dont care

1829

though a higher esteem would only produce deeper regret for her fate —
 Anne of the Mist I like not – the book I mean Arthur Philipson is what I do not like – there is an inconsistency of character —— The father is good and by & by I'll tell you what else is good and bad —— and goodbye for to night — I hope to night my soul will be gratified by one line from you — Forget me not
     Ellen T ——

[22]   (*Concord   July 1829*)
Dear Waldo
 The odourous words betrayed themselves they knew where they belonged and rested not untill they met the eye that languished for them – I hope you are not alarmed at my lady mother's nonappearance last eve – She will not go till I am firm I am not any more sick – but she wants me to be decidedly better – My first sentence must be an enigma – well then – I found out by their queer eyes that there was another letter save mine own in the house so I told them of it and told them *that* was mine too and I must see it – and now dear, good, considerate best of friends – my dear mother tells me I must give you a candid wise answer – she is sick this afternoon a debility hath seized her frame and she lifts her finger with exertion – I asked her (cruelly) to write this aft & she would

THE LETTERS

have complied to please *me* but I saw she was not able at all, at all, therefore I promised her I would write from my heart as the answer came – Now dear Waldo I have told you that mother would not come till I was really better & almost well – After you have seen my mothers face at B— I think there can be not the slightest risk in our meeting – Untill then and I could weep as I say it the danger might be great by the happening of any such mighty event or aught out of the common humdrum monotony of the last month —— There 'tis said and I sit me down content among bottles pillows and blisters smiling and looking with an eye of faith on all – and wait the coming of health & strength – they will come I believe   I do believe it sincerely – But I say *they* will come   I guess after all I must go to them – Why I think 'tis better much Waldo   to enjoy your company in one of the horrible places you describe than to leave you now – just as I begin to feel your worth – or the inestimable value of a kindred spirit – If any other means can be devised to prevent a winter of languishing and anxiety any thing suggested that says naught of seperation – how gladly would I embrace it – to be with you – and be with you in health and strength – 'tis *a blessed thought* – I feel it a hard case – Margaret is a fragile thing too – and another winter would be a tedious affair for her —— She looks so haggard and pale sometimes that I renew my solicitations for warmer climes more urgently than before ——

    Cousin Alanson is with us now and proves a house

1829

enlivener – he is a good amiable youth and will I trust be all his parents anticipate Cousin Susan says if she could only see you once she wonders who and what you are like – and sits often in deep contemplation over the miniature which she loves as the face of my *friend* and the resemblance of her cousin George ——

I hope earnestly for a letter to night – and I only wish I could write what would delight you in the least degree like the pleasure your letters give me — Good night and love me always — I dream about you again night & day ——

This was penned on Monday Aft between 5 & 6 of the o'clock —

[23] (*Concord   July 1829*)

Dear Waldo —

The house is inhabited by solemn spiritlike dancers – We meet on the stairs and greet each other with a low whisper – we pass in the entry and wink long and expressively – We glide into each other's chambers with the charitable intent of enlivening the melting hours but as we are all of the gliding race when we reach our neighbors chamber we are sure not to find them at home – they have just glided into ours – and so we meet in the entry again —— Now what an idea this must give you – of the utter vacancy of souls content to live thus inactive and sink without resistance with the body This would be making a serious matter of it – I was laughing about it when I sat down to write to you and told the girls we seemed like dancers that had wearied the musicians Since Cousins Susan and Alanson and Miss M. J. departed we have been lost so many *wet rags* together do but countenance each other in flimsiness & present a deplorable spectacle to the hearty strong natives —— Sell my wealth for a healthy winter – yes willingly – to purchase a winter of tolerable health for *one* of us —— It is a gem indeed "The gem of earthly bliss" you know Bro George calls it in his Fare-Well — dear boy! His anxiety to possess it extinguished the last and only spark that glowed to direct him to its hiding place – I read the other day the last line he wrote in his journal and he speaks of the blood feeling like melted lead in his veins ——

I have been riding in a chaise to day and Pa carried me through a green shady path in the woods   refreshing to us and heart rending to poor Jerry who despises the romance that directs us to the abode of his bitterest enemy   the gad fly – *You* fought gloriously in his behalf when we journied to Paradise and came off conqueror – But you have forgotten all that ere now —— perhaps   Well   I have nothing better to do than treasure up all these little things – I love to keep these little memories green   and I love – I love – *you*   Waldo Emerson – and I call upon you to fulfill the assurances of the note delivered at the gate of Paradise   the holy seal too – though hasty and imperfect yet strong and durable – the *impression* is still visible —— Mother is sick or I would see you

1829

soon – I think a day of cool weather will revive her *This* is debilitating to us all and this comforts me when I think of it – when she gets well she will go to Boston and then you will come here and I shall see you   I feel as if it were a twelvemonth since I had laid eyes on you ——

Good bye   I canna fash you to read such *dog-day* scrawls any more – I hope you still give me my part in the vesper service – and though last winter we found it impossible to make our "vesper bells" ring and chime together – yet we will be constant at our own hour – and constant in our hearty remembrances of each other —— God bless you   saith Ellen   or *prayeth* your own Ellen L - T   I should say ——

[24] (*Concord   July 1829*)
Dear Waldo –

Never fret yourself about me – I gain strength as fast as I can reasonably expect it – the little irregularities which are the only obstacles to perfect health will yield when the cool weather gives every body vigour and verve – My step is as firm as any of the household now and I can speak loud & clear if I could get a permit from my nurses — And I grieve if I have given you the slightest throb of anxiety by my overprudence –

Waldo   if I did not love you so well there would be not a bit of danger to see you unexpectedly any time   but you never watched the union of drops so much as I have if you do not know that at the instant

of meeting there is a universal jar – a thrill – remember and watch your window when the sky weeps ——
If I were a hundred years old and had been seperated from you a month   after living with you all my days there would be a chance of frighting the soul from the old shell when we met – by its tremour of joy perhaps – now from this intelligible sentence what do you understand   a tremour of joy in the corporeal or spiritual? – Among our many plans of *warm lodgings in Boston*   warm breezes of Cuba – mild temperatures of Washington   Baltimore, the former is most inviting surely –

Thus far had I written yesterday when I hied me to my rest and I meant to have written you a long page or two this aft — but I rode with Daddy   a 2 hours ride   and it was deemed expedient for me to give every thought a holiday and shut my dusty eyes and chain my restless tongue   and tie my truant fingers that are accused of seizing every opportu to write to Boston – now 'tis dark and I shant be at the fash of returning this in your book because it's easier to send by mail —— My dear Mother is better to day and Margaret smiles blythely ——

I love you as well to day as yesterday and am more than ever impatient to see   and good bye to you ——

[25] *(Concord   July 1829)*

My dear friend begins to stare at the alarming inconsistencies which he discovers daily in Ellinelli

1829

and why wonder? Here she is too sick to see her nearest and kindest who had been with her when she was much *sicker* and has fixed her pillows which yielded to no other hand – and yet – now she is almost well and (by her own mouth shall she be condemned) meets on the stairs every body & any body she refuses to say yea to the petition of this same dear friend to visit her —— I am well I can say – but for the strange proceedings an explanation will no doubt – will no doubt what Ellinelli? I have forgotten what I meant to say and so I will say – the nurses – the nurses – blame them — but I have made up my mind how long to wait and if they still persist I shall grow outrageous – and oh tremble ye Concordians when the ire of the Queen doth kindle against you —— Mother is better and Margaret likewise – *Boston* still is their plan — and now I'll turn newsmonger and empty the town budget – or family budget *Pa's* gone to Claremont – Rebecca is sick – Mary Jane to Claremont – and Ma is to sit tomorrow for her portrait being fascinated by the skill of that Mr Pratt who has transformed one of the most hideous of our country women into an angel of light and smiles – Margaret and Pauline talk of setting out on Tuesday next with *Sir* for Lake George – to be gone a fortnight perhaps —— Ellinelli will go to the Shakers by and by ——

The summer is fast making her parting gifts and I weep to think of her departure and to think we are doing nothing – making no preparations to accompany her — I won't say *we* – but *they* The winter (*I* ought to love it) brought me a warm friend – Should'nt whoever goes to warmer climes go as soon as the latter part of Sep? – I have taken the liberty to assert it and spur the Heads to set their house in order – I know it must be a sacrifice – for Papa especially – who finds the climate salutary and the spirits around him congenial — but if her children *must* go – Mother *will* go and if Mother goes – Father comes in as a matter of course —

Dear Waldo – I think I am foolish to prate of these things to you for as yet we can accomplish nothing and seperated or united we shall be the same true lovers ever as when we did first confess to each other and pledge an "immortal to an immortal" —— I wish I could but see you this aft ——

You write as if you *felt* musick – But I do not feel exactly so although I should imagine many would – The desire that it *creates* Good musick *satisfies* and is not wholesome food for the soul that revels in it as *I* do – It says "seek no farther" it deadens all longings for any thing better than itself – this is the character of a great part of beautiful musick though I own sometimes the soul by the stirring sentiment of the songs and a tune well adapted may be excited to nobler hopes & wishes — And it is (strange as it may appear) more apt to have this effect upon an auditor than a performer

Where are the verses that were the effect of your two favorite tunes – were they not mine? and why were they not copied immediately under your confession of their existence – Did you give them to the fair nymphs who entertained you so much to your liking? — Or did you send them to be published in Willis's periodical? – *There* how cutting!!! ——

Shall I send you this letter? No – yes – yes I will with its scratches which trouble me not they disfigure the letter but that they do take up your precious time sadly to steer between them and glean one whole, connnected, sensible thought in the whole – I have many interruptions and not infrequently a severe scolding in the midst of one of my most sentimental effusions ——

If you do not come for a week or a year you are too good & just to believe that the girl has ceased to love and confide in you – or to think that your face would be a stranger's to her – Let not such ugly thoughts ever darken your brain —— Mother will write you I think —— I love you faithfully and eternally ——

   Ellen T ——

[26]   (*Concord July 1829*)
            Tuesday aft
Dear Waldo –

I sent a letter to you last night – written on Monday – I should have dated it and have told you that Mother would stay at Miss Bacon's with Pa Kent – She cannot be persuaded to leave me for more than a day or two   and her present plan is to go down on Monday to return on Wednesday   but I hope you will all protest against it —— Boston air agrees with her & of late she has suffered from confinement & anxiety Bid her therefore that she stay a week or two ——

I recieved a letter from you last night and I am stronger and happier to day for it – Your room is my parlour and the piano   perhaps I told you   has been removed from below and stands under Grandma Tucker's portrait — this is Ellinelli's chief employ – read she cannot much   and as sure as they attempt to read to her she falls into some long dreamy labyrinth of thought and at the close is no wiser for their kindness – It is idle I know – but the flesh forbids at present greater trial of its strength —— I look with faith for sunnier hours – these are not *dark* – but a little paly –

Good night and be thinking of coming to see me some time before I go away — for I am still your own your own   your own

The sisters do often speak of you and murmer "I wish he were here"

[27]   (*Concord   July 30 1829*)

And why confess the "*magick spell*"
My love with which I bound thee?
And why my song's sweet influence tell?
The light by which I found thee?

1829

The spell is broke – and mute the voice
Which would be proud to stay thine ear
Devote itself to please thy choice
Or make the songstress self more dear

"Oft in the stilly night" my soul
Swells with remembered melody
The burst of song I scarce controul
But ah! it swells no more for me —

Is there no musick left for me?
Yes – musick that ceases but with life
                            (rather long)
Tis mine to say "I love" to thee
Tis thine to breathe the words – "my wife"
                       (only for ryhmes sake.)

Dear Waldo –
   I never compare your letters one with another the present one engrosses all my thoughts – I know not whether they have degenerated but I eat them up as they come and have relished the latter ones as much as the former – this is the truth —— Shall I find out? —— Before I forget it let me inform you that my dear Mother will go to Boston next Monday if all things are bright and fair — and if she goes to Boston on Monday and returns on Wednesday – Have I anything to hope? Now this is not because you wrote a warning but because all things are now ready ——
   Your ride to Canterbury —— How I can imagine

THE LETTERS

the sensations – I never want to hear the sound of a human voice when I revisit our dear home – but to hide in some well known spot of bushes or wander up & down silently that the ghosts of other days may come and visit me without being scared – I should not feel so strangely if all that made me happy there – were with me now – but it is so saddening yet so satisfactory a delight to live over the days again when the chain was whole!! —

I should like to see your old home I wish you could see mine as it was —— You must have laughed for joy to have found the house empty – it saved you the ugly hostile sort of feelings that fill *me* when *I* see the occupants of our mansion ——

I have ridden 9 miles this day – and the rain did its best to drive me home – but I have not taken a bit of cold and am stronger to day than I have been ever —— I have sat at the highest table once or twice but my nurses object because the baby may cry for food they think is unlawful for her to eat – and the great *exertion of self denial* in her reduced state would be too cruel —— I bless them all ——

Margaret and Paulina are well and will no doubt vouchsafe to descend when Mr Sampson appears for your sake – they always would like to be remembered to you and Mother likewise — and to your Mother Waldo do remember me when you write Good bye for the present ——

Write me some more poetry when you can – I love to read it — but spare the "women" ——

1829

Marmion is feeding beneath my window – he seems so gentle and countrified that I verily believe he would do for me to ride again – but sad to tell – we have lately discovered that he hath but one eye – and hurts himself shockingly against objects that present themselves on his dark side —— Poor Marmion! thou'rt young to lose one half of this beautiful world —— One of the squirrels is sent away – having disgraced himself by starting the colour from the queen's cheek jumping suddenly upon her and combing her locks with his horn c[omb] at the end of his paws – But Byron presses on and [wins] new laurels day by day – grows rougher in his outer man but brighter and stronger in the inner —— The white mice are as fine ladyish as ever — Felicia ah Felicia who can say where thou art lying they gave thee to be cradled by the winds and storms and snows – and none can say where thy whitened bones are now reposing or give consolation to thy bereaved mistress. So my dear friend are you not tired? and will you love me always in spite of all my nonsense and folly? — and forgive me for not dating my letters as you requested ——

This is the letter of Thursday – 5 weeks ago this blessed aft – Waldo stood by this bedside and Ellinelli blessed God who gave her such a friend.

I did not answer your question with regard to the certainty of the stage 'tis a very sure way of conveying letters and all the same to me ——

THE LETTERS

[28] (*Concord, Aug. 1829*)

I thank you for your letter of last night – and now dont be alarmed at the showers of scrawls which you recieve weekly, daily, hourly. Write I must but read you need not every day – wait till I come to Boston – and we'll set down and read them together ——

The weather is delicious and I have ridden again to day – and am stronger of limb and clearer in head than yesterday — getting well – getting well —— Never was person more favored – there is nothing that I need so much as an increase of the sense of it — I talk about it and cant help it — but bitterly it comes over me that when I am free and every hour has its own gratification my thoughts will refuse to bear on their wing the sense of the never failing goodness of my God. I wonder I will do so – sometime I think I had rather not get well than to be sure with returning health to experience returning thoughtlessness —— If firm resolution can do aught and fervent prayer I will resolve and pray — and do thou *for* me my own dear friend ——

The mother will come soon yet often saith – for why? I say for good — If I get well I shall be *very very* strongly tempted to go with her — I guess she winna let me and it is well – *well* on some accounts – ill, ill on many ——

You are a good boy – and Good bye to you saith
Ellen T——

1829

This was written at 5 o'clock on Thursday aft nursey preparing my supper and Paulina watching the spirit departing out of a snake —— Margaret absorbed in Anne of the Mist —

[29] *(Concord. Aug. 1829)*

Here is my last pure bit of paper and at present I can command no more but luckily I am not in the fit much or I should pout that I lacked room for the effusions of my boiling-over brain —— My head is murky like the sky this aft and I have done little to day but walk round to search for a gleam of sunshine —— "No letters" said Harvey last night – I frowned but nobody saw me 'twas so dark —— Here's a bundle for you said the fellow this morning – I laughed outright and for sympathy's sweet sake so did he —— I hope you do not write to me when you should be trying to out-dream Charles —— Sleep must be your strength and I hope you do not steal hours from it – I have experienced or I do experience so much kindness and attention daily that I fear I shall grow selfish and recieve it as the beggars in Concord do money as their due —— Do you not love *me* too well I shall say to sacrifice your health? ——

I am *very very* stupid and know I shall but write follity if I try to write a long page – strange to tell I believe every word you say whether it be concerning your soul or body – and if you start and apologize for the use of the deep expression who use it so seldom what shall I plead to convince you that my frequent use of it is heartfelt always —— My soul has been my intimate for a good while and oh to my shame be it known how little I really know it I love you from & with *my soul* – and would with my heart likewise if I were its mistress – but it is thine ——

Waldo was back in Concord by August 6th, and the next day he and Ellen in the chaise, and Mrs Kent in a covered vehicle with the baggage, started on a ten-day excursion to the White Mountains. They visited the Shaker community at Canterbury, Centre Harbor on Lake Winnipesaukee, Conway, and Bartlett, returning by way of Plymouth, Orford, and Hanover. Ellen stayed well. In a letter to Mrs. Lyman on August 26th, Waldo says of the trip: "You will not forgive me if I shd. omit to tell you that Miss Ellen Tucker is a good deal better for being jounced over two hundred miles of hard ground in N. Hampshire lately. We went in a chaise to the Notch of the White Hills. Mrs Kent went in a carriage as a safe resort in case of showers or sickness but Ellen did not once enter it." Waldo returned to Boston on August 19th.

[30] *(Concord Aug 1829)*
                                        Thursday aft —
Dearest Waldo,

I hope ere this you have embraced your good brother and slumbered on your ain bed —— Time lags wearily and I think of you *all the time*. Wherefore are we seperated? says my lonely heart — I am not complaining – no, not a bit — but it is rather delightful to me the progress our affection has made — wrapping us more closely every day in its fairy web of smiles and tears. We have tried a short journey together and like so well that we think of taking a *longer* —. If we meet with as few streams to ford   as few hard hills to climb   as many good friends   and *as few hangers on* shall we not be fortunate? ———

I did as I was bid and Mother went with me to the New Road woods which we penetrated to the end thereof   many delicate strangers we found in the thickest part and I gathered them to ascertain when I got home their names and places of residence but they died before I could find them   and Death so marred their loveliness that their very near and dear kindred would not have recognized them — the sighing pines are pretty though they be of Concord growth and breathe Concord air —— I am writing by way of relief to my thoughts.

I have but a moment to speak to you now for after debating a long while whether you would thank me for such a scrawl I have concluded to trust to your goodness and forbearance

I don't want Mother to write to Mr Cutler   she says you told her it would please you   I winna, I canna, I munna, I shall not consent to it – only let us wait a bit — till the girls arrive —— I have been through brier and brake again this aft   obtained no hair of pity for scratches and weaknesses   they all *go to make me sleep* – I hope you will tell me of the state of your heart in your next – I forbear to flutter you with hopes of the verdure of mine —— Ellen is yours if her pen will only allow her to write it intelligibly

THE LETTERS

—— I shall look with longing eyes for the letter Pst ——

[31] (*Concord. Aug. 1829*)

After a battle of words with the blundering Jackson Postmaster and after convincing him that I knew better about the matter than he did Harvey brought your letter which is quietly at rest with its fellows after being perused and reperused till it is written on my eyeballs – this is Saturday my dear friend   the sun rises & sets   the stars and moon are as luminous as erst the wind blows hot & cold   though Waldo & Ellen after spending a happy fortnight together are parted —— My fingers are more sympathetic – they refuse to move briskly and my tongue   that *little helm* which under good government saveth the ship so many dangers   will not obey me – The maiden apart from her lover – is an insulated being – she misseth the welcome tones which no other instrument can afford her   the sweet attentions which no other hand will or *shall* render her – her tale findeth no vent in words – the moon is but a chill confident and of all the strange secrets that she is possessed of – she never revealeth one or returneth confidence for confidence ——

Mother strictly obeys your parting injunction and perpetual motion is her theme – she whirls me in the carriage to Hopkinton and she whirls me into the

1829

woods on my toe – the inhabitants of Concord can scarce say lo here or lo there before we are far beyond their power and calls, parties, and compliments, glance by unoticed —— I rejoice you are yet to behold William and in your good tidings of Edward — Nay – I was not a bit jealous that I should be surplanted in your heart by the number (or any one of the number I mean) who claim yours as a kindred soul – I tell you Waldo *I* am the nearest link in the chain to your heart – if you have *kindred* spirits beside – then I am your *own spirit* – I am I say – I *will be* I should say —— The new influence is the sole one of the kind —— Do you shake your head in unbelief? — and so you deny me the priviledge of being the ewe lamb —— This is all for the sake of prattling a little longer you will think but I am serious ——

Oh what a robin sung there! — he has been warbling to me all the while I have been writing I guess he sends greeting to you – Well my sweet songster – I am in no danger from you – as much love and beauteous harmony as you can spare I will send ——

The shakers have not sent for me yet when the bretheren come down perhaps they will reserve a seat for me ——

Mothers love is abundant towards you – from the sisters we hear nothing — if the *gross realities* increase as they journey north they will be glad to come back again —

THE LETTERS

Will you be pleased to think of me often and love me always —— thine dear Waldo ever ——

Ma has not written to Pa Cutler on the ugly subject yet nor do I mean to have her *s'il vous plait* ——

Que – What is an island?
Ans – An island is a portion of land entirely surrounded by water —
Que – Define the word – insulated –
Ans – Island fashion —
[*The next three lines are crossed out completely*]

[32]   (*Concord   Aug. 25 1829*)
Dear Waldo

Such a cloud of stupidity never rested on a poor body's skull as hangs this blessed moment over mine – whether it be the wilfulness of the crimson tide that will gang its ain gait or the *muggy* sullen air I know not all I care about it is that I should take such an opportunity to write to your grace and suffer the droppings of the cloud to annoy my best friend —— 'Tis often thus our love for our friends seldom makes us too disinterested to gratify old misery in her love of company and make them partakers of our woes if we can ——

The intelligence your letter bears is fair – Mother is pleased I think with the prospect for the winter Mrs K. would I suppose deny us 5 *rooms* if the girls

1829

should happen to fancy boarding there – it would be desirable if she could grant them to persuade them to winter with us on many accounts – We heard from them last night and they are probably now at L. George from whence they will write again – Pa mentions their visit to the Cathedral at Montreal – but speaks disappointedly I think – generally the interior of such buildings is more splendid than the ex – but this is not so – I should think from his description it was like a childs self made toy – in the ardour of the first novelty of the thing he works with nicety and beauty but grows slacker as this ceases and the *"last end* of that toy shall be worse than the first"

But the burden of your letter shall not be neglected in mine – Woe betide the eye that would peep under the said blanket of uncertainty – "For under that black veil a darker veil   Still threatening to defy me stretches wide" It matters little whether we know or not – but that plan which has been convulsing the wise heads   oh! how droll   how infinitely laughable!

—— Mother never seemed to like it – and would only do it to please *you* – glad am I that you   being a babe in such things   will resign them to more experienced noddles and I thank you ——

I saw the golden rod and the aster yesterday in the Abbot Woods – the golden rod is a flower, a flower, that, that, but perhaps you've seen it – it waves sweetly — I thought of you in those woods and the crows helped me for they held their "sour converse in the sky" — I would not talk scandal or I might have ill will for you — Waldo – I want to see you more than ever heart longed for another after a weeks absence before —— The story has flown from lip to lip of our anticipated – anticipated what? union – that is foolish too – no matter – and Concord folks grin as if they were indebted to you for the removal of a well known scold or some such calamity —— They wont be kept in the dark they bring in their own lights if one wont help them to any ——

I am sorry William Emerson has not arr'd yet —— But does'nt he write or give reasons for his delay? I trust you will soon see him and have chats long and merry as brothers & sisters delight to — Oh what a sweet tie – what a blessed one ——

I am going to walk now – when I return if the light favours me I will write you some more but if it is late I shall only sign my name to the assertion that my love forever burneth From heaven it came to heaven returneth

Our walk has been beautiful but long and my spirit will participate I trust tomorrow in the glow of my renewed bodily strength I love you Ralph Waldo Emerson dearly Ellen L T

[33] (*Concord. Aug. 1829*)

I wish you were here – heartily wish it – and you now need wait no permit – come when you can – 1 week and 2 whole days have sailed by since our

1829

seperation and weeks and months never have seemed so long to me as now —— My little cousin Mary has arrived and she prattles the livelong day – striving to make me laugh and to entertain herself with my "solemncholic phiz" – I tell the little gipsey "I laugh in my sleeve very often" but she thinks it's more becoming to wear smiles upon the lips for she says she loses a common laugh in the immensity of silk folds in the bishop sleeves – Come soon and see me I know of some beautiful walks – carpetted walks – no Brussels or Turkey half so soft to the feet as my (our) parlour is furnished with – I should love to hear you bid the "proud world Goodbye" there – verily after walking in these woods an hour or so – I sicken to come out in the broad bold light and hear and see the busy *world's* people — You see I shall do better than ever for the wooden cup and white handkerchief – I'll wait till yr next visit before I assume them –

We had tidings of M & P last night – tomorrow they may come home but more probably not till Monday. I long to see them – Pa excused M's neglect in not writing on account of extreme lassitude —— Long journeys are bad for the frail gauze flower I'm afraid – or she travels too fast and thoughtlessly. They have been far with sunny havens and good weather for water travelling but the dust has annoyed them I suspect in stages. Oh yes I am glad we have done with the ugly *insurance* business – bad on every account – Mother never liked it I raved about it – and so would my good free hearted sisters if they ever thought or heard of it —— Dont you scare Pa Cutler by the mention of such a thing   he is so *very very* anxious to do right   and *carefully*   that I would not – you'd only give him a black thing to plague him whereas now the good man owns how fair our earthly prospects are — how good is my companion etc   I know he'd say   yes! and for worlds I would not have him —— He would think you were doubting *yourself* and would be justified in doubting too ——

Write to Pa just so as the scheme says – I think he will yeild and be glad to live with his *better half* on these terms – Rebecca will be married and I have small doubts of the other one's prospects — the girls I mean Paulina and Margaret will of course be at B and I hope with us or near us – 'tis better we live together that we see the same things and grow into one another — one heart the Siamese boys have between them   I suppose – connected more firmly in spirit than in flesh –

Come and mend me some pens for your own sake. Your N.H. map is safe in my porte-folio – strange for such an useful thing to 'scape this bottomless pit — I saw Dobbin with his master on his back yesterday – but he refused to acknowledge me – his fellow traveller   by bow or sign – Proff Carter has rode Marmion every day for sometime and says he is a fine horse – having no great fault in him. He has shut one eye against the world but how much more merit   no doubt it is employed usefully within the house –

Waldo Emerson   hear how a maiden loves you –

1829

better than earthly hope or object – faithfully – purely – wonder not at her boldness of speech but recieve her words as her heart-drops – Good bye –

I am hushed in my usual complaints of the approaching fall of the beauty of nature Our love blossoms in autumn – henceforth I'll love the autumn

My confession shows through the paper distinctly and I must write this over to hide it from curious eyes – Mary Jane has gone with *Job* to ride   her regards are often yours but I forget to send them ——

[34]   *(Concord, Aug. 30 1829)*
                    Tuesday aft —
Dear Waldo —

The sparkle of meeting is hardly over and the sisters tales so marvellous are yet but half exhausted But I canna be so happy all alone – You must joy with me in their restoration and I'll treasure up for you all that delights my ear and eye —— Margaret is improved by her journey and Paulina is full of life and very happy —— The daddy is hugging himself and his dear Pegg – looks younger and not so *homely* —— The letter if written had better be aimed and fired as soon as suits your Grace's convenience —— He the disbeliever told Margaret that he was confident we should not live together this winter ——

I forget but I think you must have had a letter from me on Saturday – I seem to be writing or talking to you all the time – The "ever present thought" I can echo heartily. Few, let them love ever so ardently and purely have the happiness to lie down in the earth together – The hand of Death while it destroys one, merely numbs (chills) the other as warning or *a comfort* – and the tearless eye and the hopeful peaceful smile serve to show the confidence, and affection the unwavering trust in Heaven still unabated *and what true Love is*. In that sort of affection there can be no hypocrisy – And the worst heart would not doubt the purity thereof —— Let us love thus, Oh my good Waldo, I believe we do now and we need not be united to increase our affec – "A sea" — Surely!! — *whose waters cast up pearls and gems* –

The foilage of the New Road woods still successfully waves in invitation to mother & self and is still so good as to keep up its pride and not make the humiliating offer of itself for our carpet —— We sit upon a large log every aftn and like two owls fall to winking and thinking as if the weighty affairs of a nation encumbered us —— Verily I rejoice that I can make one beautiful exception when I rave of blazing heats and reflecting sands ——

You will come soon – and a warm welcome how needless to promise you – I wish I knew what your eye rests upon this minute (nearly 3 o'clock) — it pleases me often to think we must chance to wake and sleep at the same time – Why don't our fancies meet when they wander in dreams – Mayhap they do. Oh the pleasing perplexing labyrinths ——

1829

Only come – Last night I recd your letter and the bundles all are safe – but the journals are dangerously sick, many infirmities of old age press upon them and their end is near – be not down-cast if they have departed this life ere you arrive and the beautiful ashes be all that is left for your longing eye to rest upon. How like the thousand other traces of dear hours – I prefer and so would you if you were Ellen Tucker to have no record so distinct of the past — how much better to view all of it "Pictured in memorys mellowing glass" – But   Oh for me   though it cost you a laugh   save me what I do want and crave most ardently as I love you   I speak truly and sincerely ——

Good bye and you will know that I love you better than ever when we meet – for you will never disbelieve me – again I was tempted to write   but no! 'tis past all doubt — Yes am I ever ——
Ellen T ——

[35]   *(Concord, Sept. 4, 1829)*
Dear Waldo,

Are you sad that I have written you but once before this week   I'm sad to think o't but neglectful you cannot believe me – my excuses shall be whispered in your own ear next week – meanwhile I beg your Lordship's clemency —— And I thank you for all I have recieved and the good news therein contained   What can make you tell fairy tales to Wil-

THE LETTERS

liam? his eyes will search in vain for the brilliant object you have described to him – If tales must be told how much better to tell him she was insensible and wretchedly deformed than to subject him to such a disagreeable disappointment – I think I must ask M.J. to feign herself the *one* and present herself in her radiance as his sister and I as a *sister* of the *sister* might pass ——

Dear Waldo, I anticipate another week with you with the most gleeful heart – we can be nearer though so very, very near – we can be dearer though it seems sometimes as I loved you *much too well* for my own happiness of mind – no I dont mean *happiness* I mean *welfare*, health of soul, —— Dobbin waits our pleasure but he wont like to go to Bristol – however we will talk these matters over when we meet ——

Wo! Wo! for these ruthless winds they sweep o'er my heart strings making most melancholy musick —— Winter seems already to be come upon us – and some of my beautiful sweet peas regret their love of life and the tenacity with which they have clung to it and are now bending pale & withered over the beds of their long ago departed kindred or all colourless & nipped they are standing still upright and shivering in the wind —— Oh Bermuda sigh we all — Oh Cuba — Oh St Augustine ——

I am glad William wants a watch guard & such as I can I will give him with joy – but Concord affords but rough materials for such little niceties when I come to Boston if this looks ugly I'll make him a better one

1829

—— Have I written to you since I heard you were coming   I believe I have not — though 'tis foolish to waste time to say you welcome —— I have just recd a letter from Eliz Sparhawk   she writes darkly and sullenly for her – The family will remove to Conway next summer and she seems to think she wishes nothing better if God will spare her father's life and peace of mind —— I love her well – *she* deserveth the name of *queen* truly – "a queenly soul in a queenly case" — this you have yet to learn —— Paulina Tucker is sick today and Margaret unco' blythe — Mother is very very well   eke daddy —— oh you have recd the letter from him – you will have tonight — He doubted its requiring an answer but I insisted it did —— I hear that one *very decided* step has been taken with regard to our winter prospects – a little bird from B. came with the *publick* news of our "intended marriage" – but that's nothing at all – we may *not* as we may — No I dont mean it is as probable but as possible – Ah you dinna ken how such a nestling as I have been feels in her soul at the change of prospect. A nestling I still shall be I know – and change a cold but half acknowledged home for a dear, warm, faithful *home* – but I may be a mere nothing for a year to come – a being of perfect dependance — not fit to perform the every day offices of love and friendship for any of my friends — I do not repine that I am thus but I shall blame myself if I do [*torn*]ce myself where I shall be – Good bye friend [Waldo]   I always get so puzzled to express what I want to say that I never can

THE LETTERS

try again —— I love you and will always — if I cannot express nor you imagine the little dark shadows why I will trust where they are known and understood. To your mother always give my love – to William and Charles always remembrances —— Monday night do not forget that you will be anxiously expected by your own Ellen T ——

O forgive the nonsensical stuff – it was there and to whom but you should it be spoken —— Friday

Dont you tease for papers or journals & such like when you come – wait till October ——

Waldo returned to Concord again on September 7th, and there was an excursion with Mrs. Kent and Margaret. They drove to Worcester, Springfield, where Waldo preached two sermons, and Hartford. On the fifteenth, Waldo wrote to Abel Adams from Worcester on the way back: "The weather has been extremely favourable for our ride & 'the winds of heaven have been tempered to the shorn lamb' — Ellen has borne all extremely well, & appears much stronger; & except a damp morning & one or two piecings out of our journey after dark – has ridden always in the chaise. Margaret & Mrs Kent in the carriage . . . We travel for air & jolting & and these we have gotten & our own company was sufficiently good. Books we carry, & at the taverns we read and scribble — but not sermons."

This poem and the next one are copied into R.W.E.'s journal, and dated at Pepperell, Massachusetts, September 1829. It seems probable that they represent some of the verses they scribbled, and that Pepperell was one of their stopping-places.

Dear Ellen, many a golden year,
May ripe, then dim, thy beauty's bloom,
But never shall the hour appear
In sunny joy, in sorrow's gloom,
When aught shall hinder me from telling
My ardent love, all loves excelling.

The spot is not in the rounded earth,
In cities vast, in islands lone,
Where I will not proclaim thy worth,
And glory that thou art mine own;
Will you, nill you, I'll say I love thee
Be the moon of June or of March above thee.

And when this porcelain clay of thine
Is laid beneath the cold earth's flowers,
And close beside reposes mine,
Prey to the sun and air and showers,
I'll find thy soul in the upper sphere,
And say I love thee in Paradise here.

I call her beautiful; — she says
Go to! your words are idle;
My lips began to speak her praise,
My lips she tried to bridle.
But, Ellen, I must tell you this,
Your prohibition wasted is,
Unless among your things you find
A little jail to hold the mind;
If you should dazzle out mine eyes,
As dimmer suns sometimes have done,
My sleepless ears, those judges wise,
Would say, 'Tis the voice of the Peerless One.
And if your witchery decree
That my five senses closed should be,
The little image in my soul
Is Ellen out of Ellen's controul,
And whilst I live in the universe
I will say 'tis my beauty, for better, for worse.

1829

They were back in Concord September 17th, and Waldo went to Boston the following day.

[36]   *(Concord   Sept. 1829)*
Dear Waldo,
    You have had a golden day for your departure and the sun is smiling its last most sweetly at this moment – the memory of our beautiful last acquaintance filleth me, so that I scarce believe you are gone – the Last man, the Rainbow, Byron's best   to say nothing of certain ryhmes to my ear fuller, richer, weightier by far than either   I cherish most fondly for they echo within me yet —— Your books have feasted me too this day   truly   Waldo Emerson   they delight me — place not a barrier between us or think that the deepest you write is altogether incomprehens   to me — they will be useful to me such as these – give me more I pray of you – As to papers you will be poorly paid for I can find but here & there a stray bit for you — but you ken we are to live together   and I will see if I cant write some more one of the long days in winter — and I do dearly love you — yea better & better   and the words grow more & more expressive & solemn —— *God bless you* Waldo

[37]   *(Concord Sept   1829)*
Dear Waldo —
    I hope this beautiful bland day reaches you – and you rejoice in its light as I do —— I have proved this

day that my feet like Miss Polly Dolly Adelaide's were made to use and the good folks of Concord cease to stare for the *publishment* they think is reason enough for running —— *Why* & wherefore did I not write you last night? – because Mr Lathrop of Dover spent the evening with us and the dad and Marm called me from my snug corner to entertain him – But you should have heard Sat night – and tonight is the night I am to have a letter – I trust you will not disappoint me – so darkly do the days roll when I have no communication with you   Waldo Emerson   that time is to me as if it had never been and a blot is the record of my *mourning* days — How bright will the days be when we cannot be seperated [*sketch of scissors*]   We will have a clock like the one Mrs H. sings of – where time is noted by the opening and closing flowers —

I heard from Pauline Saturday night   she will stay she says till the latter part of this week. I hope Mrs Keating can accomodate them both   or someone who lives near Chardon St —— Chardon St? for why? what have Miss Tuckers to do with Chardon St – why Waldo Emerson   a friend of Ellen Tucker's will board there and they would all like to be near him ——

I have very little to say to you but the main thing remains unsaid — and let me assure you now of the unalterable state of my affections   of the indwelling love of the deep & deepning interest I feel for you – who can boast such a golden *courtship*   who can enjoy such bright anticipations? ——

1829

    I shall write you I guess tomorrow – woe betide you if tonight brings no tidings —
    I wish Aunt Mary's letter would come – Is't not on the road – Margaret is reading the new novel and has just looked up to sigh —
    Fare thee well – I'm sorry my song is so very unmusical this aft – ever thine
E T

Dear Waldo here it is nearly 10 o'clock and my letter I have forgotten to send – I have just remembered you in my vespers and I hope I shall be with you in dreams this night

I shall send by the stage ——   Monday night

[*On the outside of the paper:*] I have just recd yours and am happy

[38]   (*Concord   Sept 25, 1829*)
Dear Waldo ——
    You begin to wonder where are my black scrawls I suppose and conjecture many naughty things —— My words shall be few this aft for I am getting well of an ailing stomach and a troublesome thing it has been though not a bit alarming – but I mean to keep well therefore am I mighty tender of mind and body and you shall see me as well as when you left if possible —— I tell you Waldo Emerson you must not

leave off writing me when we live together – I love such long lived lines of affection – and your last letter gave me such a hopeful peaceful, happy, joyous hour as I never find anything else can produce and such as I am very, very grateful for —— For *my sake* I would say – let us die together but the world is (leanly) scantily furnished with such as thou art (tell it not in Gath) and honestly —— no! I wont but I hope we both shall live long enough to do much good in every way – to suffering soul and aching body —— but stop – let us live together first – and then we will talk about the rest — only be sure and keep writing – What a pity I canna write a farewell – but all I love dearly will be with me – and in this sandy desert no little green spot presents its radiant eye for a parting tribute The children who grieve a wee bit now will laugh as brightly no doubt (I hope) an hour after our chaise hath rolled away – no body but Grandma and Granpa Meserve that has displayed any *inspiring* regrets or poetical depth of feeling ——

Byron speaks not at parting but his whole countenance at meeting is eloquent – I like it of him – parting is a dread dark uncertain form – meeting is a *sure bright* joyful visitation —— We close the lids of our eyes as emblematical of our blindness – of our shortsightedness When *we* part we are sure almost sure that we have one bright streak for our own in the path before us an enduring evergreen that will border our way.

I love you Waldo most dearly and this is the

1829

last time I shall write it to you   I trust   from wont of a nearer communi
   Yes   I am ever faithfully
      Ellen T ——

Take care of your knee   do,   don't leave the docter's wing because you have promised to be here   Obey ——

I must weave a veil for the postmaster's eyes [*torn*] *hot lead* as this must not be risked again – Bid sister P[aulina] return   do   and tell her I send her much love   and Cousin Mary has been sick again   but is better now and wants to see her —— Waldo   I care not a whit about the parlour   I said upper because I must say something but my heart is less wild than formerly and I care not ——

PART TWO

DECEMBER 1829 — FEBRUARY 1831

Ralph Waldo Emerson and Ellen Louisa Tucker were married at the Kent mansion in Concord on September 30th, 1829. On October 4th they settled down in lodgings at Mrs. Keating's, Chardon Street, Boston. The Kents and Margaret and Paulina were also boarding there. Waldo's letters and journals indicate a happy domestic life. A letter to Aunt Mary Moody Emerson is the only surviving one of Ellen's during this period. Ellen must have been very curious about Waldo's aunt. The only letter that exists to her from Aunt Mary had been written in January 1829, when Ellen was in Boston after the engagement had been announced. The greater part of this letter follows; there is no beginning and no signature, and notes to Waldo are written on the back: "As soon as I read your character – lovely Louisa   I could do nothing but commend you to God – and pray that you might be a lasting blessing to him it is your favored lot to attach. Yes   highly favored   I may well say, not because he is a relative (that is distant and less than ever I expect any intercourse with him) but I know his temper . . . But why are you in the city? They will buz to you of musick – of literature – of chemistry – of everything that will disturb the culture of your *character* – everything averse to that enthusiasm or piety or extensive benevolence or high-minded principles which can alone support devotion to God —— *Do not read everything*. Let Law's 'Serious Call' be ever on your table and 'Night tho'ts'. These will inevitably form you to rational and fervent religion. Do you love works of fiction – let Flora MacIvor, Jenny Deans, Corinne, and the full portrait of Moore's [*illegible*] be before you. The man that God has blest you with is devoted to the highest and most urgent office. Lean not on him for resources – but urge him on to aid in the work of moral improvement which is going on for Heaven. Be yourself a ministering angel to him and society. You no more than others can ever love virtue practically till it costs you something. Jenny Deans is a masterpiece for illustrating the morale of religion. I hope you don't paint nor talk french.

Hope you'll be a unique. And *love* poetry – that musick of the soul."

Ellen's letter is addressed to "Miss Mary Emerson, Greenfield, Mass.," and is endorsed in R.W.E.'s writing. "Ellen Tucker E. 1829." It was probably written in December. There is a notation in M.M.E.'s writing, "Dear gone Ellen's."

[39] *(Ellen Tucker E. 1829)*

Dear Aunt Mary,

I've had a letter written to you this great while which the blessings & changes of every day removed farther & farther from the truth – I tell you of Waldo's lameness there – of Charles absence – and of Edward's long silence —— I rejoice to tell you *now* of Waldo's complete recovery to wholeness of Charles's return of Edward's good health and of the actual presence of my dear mother in the city — I fear e'en now I shall have been anticipated in my histories and my tardiness in answering your queries and acknowledging your kind remembrances and gratulations must most justly be censured — But *Exercise – Exercise* is the command and I strictly obedient to all such, unless I can write walking or riding, must burden my friends with sleepy words or cease all intellectual exercise – It seems to write to *you* like a person born blind & conversing with a dear friend ——

I have heard from many tongues of Aunt Mary from many more of "Mary Emerson" – yet have at every mention of you made some alteration in my

1829

ideal Aunt Mary and now as I write a thousand differing forms of you keep crossing my brain ——

I am indeed no common object for sympathy – I feel all efforts weak at congratulations – and the more as my days go by – and now the deepest and most impressive are *far far* from reaching that chord which is trembling with its own impatience to be heard and touched into expression —— Rosy hours perchance *all* may experience – a *rosy life* falls to few ——

You will not forget how much we want you to come and see us before you go home — Waldo would join with me in love if he knew of the opportunity to send —— Your new niece
Ellen T.

William is in Boston and brings glad tidings from Edward – he will stay only a day or two —

R.W.E. copied these verses into one of his Blotting Books, dating them February 26th, 1830.

And, Ellen, when the greybeard years
Have brought us to life's evening hour,
And all the crowded Past appears
A tiny scene of sun and shower,

Then, if I read the page aright
Where Hope, the soothsayer, reads our lot,
Thyself shalt own the page was bright,
Well that we loved, wo had we not;

When Mirth is dumb and Flattery's fled,
And mute thy music's dearest tone,
When all but Love itself is dead,
And all but deathless Reason gone.

1830

The threat of ill health still hung over Ellen, and in March 1830 Waldo took her and Margaret to Philadelphia to try a change of climate. At Hartford, on the way, he had preaching engagements, and he was eager to introduce Ellen to Aunt Mary, who was boarding in Wethersfield at the time. Ellen described the meeting with Aunt Mary in a rhymed journal of the trip. Aunt Mary wrote to her nephew Charles on March 15th about Ellen: "I like her better than I dreamt — but not near so handsome – genius and loveliness are enough."

Ellen's journal, labeled "Philadelphia Journal," consists of sixteen small pages, and was written, or rather scribbled, as they went along. Most of it was written by Ellen, but several times Waldo took over and added his impressions. There are unfinished bits and much crossing out. The sections omitted here are those that are incomplete or obscure — comments on people and places that doubtless made sense to Ellen, Waldo, and Margaret, but not to anyone else.

[40] [*March 1830*]

The Philadelphia Journal

    Youth and the opening rose
    May look like things too glorious for decay
    But thou art not of those
    Who wait the ripened bloom to seize their prey.

    "A boat, a boat to cross the ferry
    For we're a-ganging to be merry
    To laugh & quaff & drink good sherry."

THE PHILADELPHIA JOURNAL

[*March 9, 1830*]

At Framingham last Tuesday night
My muses had deserted quite,
And I like babe in all but size
Used nothing but my tongue and eyes.
To Worcester next morn at 5
I stupid murmur "caught alive" –
We started and arrived at 10
There spent the day – Well Marm what then –
What then? Why we to Springfield speeded
Nor mud nor hour late we heeded,
Thoughts of Aunt Mary long desired
And pillows downy   fires glowing
Keep us from plaints of being tired,
And our good will and humour flowing.
O Springfield ne'er to be forgotten
Famous for promises all rotten
3 hours of time to us thou'rt owing
Before we're gone – gone, going, going.
Arrived at Morgans palace fine
By Hartford clocks at ½ past 9.

Saturdays sun hath wrapped his form
In flannels gauze and vapours warm.
Waldo to Weathersfield did ride,
And to my joy I soon espied
Him homeward bound – & by his side
Aunt Mary's eyes her niece did scan
Compared it with her previous plan,

1830

The building was not half so fine
Nor did the painted windows shine
As her fond fancy nursed his lies,
But hard enough to like she tries
To faults determined closed her eyes
And wouldn't mind them —

[*R.W.E. continues; at Hartford, where he preached three sermons, on March 14:*]
Sunday we went or some of us did
To Allynes Hall since the Church was forbid
Believing all places are open to Heaven
And a church of seven thousand no better than seven
But the minister preached as well as he could
And he hoped   not knew   that he was understood
But I wish we could carry the keeping of Sunday
To something more than the washing day habits of Monday
Be as good as our sires a hundred years back
Who kept the Connecticut Blue Laws or Black
For who keeps Sunday in heart and holdeth his tongue
Is surely better than he who acts so as to deserve to be hung.

[*Ellen continues on Tuesday:*]
We went to walk and view the charms
Of New Haven's city farms
Many splendid houses rise
Many bookstores greet our eyes

Many blue cloaked sons of science
But we bid them all defiance
And with sauntering idle look
Critic's observation took.
Darkly did this night shut down
Above us clouds of winds are forming
I'm convinced it will be storming
Heigh ho for a week at New Haven town.

At 6 our eyelids broke
The seal of nights impression
And in haste we woke
For fear of a transgression
On the steamboat's hours
Though the morn was lowering
Better go when it pours
Than sit here a cowering.
Who that had good feet
Who that owned a shilling
In a stage to get a seat
To be soaked in a boat is willing.
Found at last 'twas vain
Trying to cross all sound
What to do was plain
Make for nearer ground.
Here we sit and here
We must sit & talk
For 'tis very clear
We can't ride Norwalk.
O the delight of spending a night

1830

On board of a steam *packet*
Down below, grovelling woe,
Above, cold rain and racket.
Morn came at last on us as we lay
Anchored in rocking majesty
Like conquerors tho' we proudly moved
Across the half appeased sea
That still kept muttering peevishly
Like babe refused the toy it loved.
We gain & now as if to smile
On hands & hearts unwearied yet
Old Sol his cold reserve forgets
And doth our widowed hearts beguile
Or else in fleeing through the sky
He lost his mantle off by chance
And pitied as he cast his eye
On each wet woeful countenance
So for the present laid it by.

We're here, we're here and spires tall
And buildings of a busy world
And people like the emmet small
And mud and finery together hurled.
Glad were we when our bodies laid
On beds that under us would stay
And glad were we to greet once more
Smiles and kind glances seen before.

   [*R.W.E. continues:*]
O Broadway   O Broadway   where beauty parades

THE PHILADELPHIA JOURNAL

In the splendor of paint, lace, plumes, flowers &
 brocades
O Broad way of fashions & broadway of trades
My mind is unequal thy pomp to unfold
Thy wealth & thy folly, noise, motion, & gold
 Howbeit thy beaux
 Made me turn up my nose
 And if I told my sincere tho't
 I fear that thy belles would love me not –

[*Ellen continues:*]
But still the impartial sun on thee
Shed its bright ray as pleasantly
As if the glittering gems & flowers
Were gifts from Nature's richest bowers
And to the riding school of York
We steered upon the rough stone walk
But neither equestrian skill
Nor waving splendours tempt our will
To swerve from this till we grow stronger
We'll brave this blue east wind no longer
So I will end the song & tell
Of dining late at the Hotel
And after dinner sitting down
Like wondering eager new come clown
And blushing like a country miss
To see the utter nakedness
And how they cheat the legs of clothes
While the long arms in state repose.
Farewell   tomorrow's dawning day

1830

Will find us bounding on our way
Hurrah for Philadelphia
Saturday
Goodbye, Goodbye   now noise beginning
Hark! the parting bell is ringing
Fare thee well and in
   [*R.W.E.'s writing starts:*] a whistle
We left the wharf on board the Thistle
Swept o'er the wide bay – Who but we!
Threaded the inlands merrily
And after breakfast we began
To ascend the muddy Raritan.

   [*Ellen continues from Philadelphia:*]
Fair land of bonnets white and neat
Of taste so pure   of streets so clean
That here the first pigs we have seen
Lay wallowing in thy muddy streets
Thy spotless fame will melt away
Beware   Oh Philadelphia!!!
With bag and baggage all pell mell
We rode to the U.S. Hotel
And having found good chambers two
And pleasant beds & rest in view
We thought we'd stay till we should find
Some lodgings suited to our mind
But by the way – without a jest
In *P*   the wind is sometimes East.
Sunday   [*March 21*]
Mild zephyrs welcomed us this morn

And springs first beauties seemed to dawn
A Sunday calm and cool and bright
A day of pure unclouded light
No meeting goers we to day
Though Waldo goodly showed the way.
Monday
Another day of beauty rare
Another heaven of earth & air
We found a boarding house at last
Though our researches first were vast
But Mrs McElroy did offers make
Of parlour chamber we of course must take
So we tomorrow lift once more our feet
To set them firmly on Eleventh St.
Here are we lodged – and here are like to stay
Till one of us three crows do fly away
Or till the beauteous thriving month of May.
And Oh how stiff and madamish we sit
Nor joke nor bend in dignity a bit
For here are gentilhommes one, 2, 3, 4,
And when he's well there will be yet 1 more.
Wednesday
All nature smiled fair when I my eye
Oped on this globe's light and shade
And as I mused so thoughtfully
My sight this strange discovery made
A little insect rich & red
With our own hearts blood on the blanket played
In scorn I slew him in his downy bed
I pray he may not haunt me with his shade –

1830

Well! charity – we'll to the hall descend
And our bad spirits with some breakfast mend
A well spread table does the dame display
Neat though not rare & splendid – in its way.
On Saturday Old Boreas' roar
Was heard in whistles bold
He shook the spindling poplars more
Than I could well unfold
He played the rogue with every feather
And mingled love and rage together
For often like *young* love he'd seem
And whisper gauze-like Fancy's dream
Then like *Old love's* reality
In earnest prove himself to be.

[*March 28*]

Sunday   To church twice strayed our feet.
Monday   This day's a box of roses sweet.

[*End of Journal*]

On March 25th, 1830, R.W.E. started a letter to his brother Charles, who was living at Abel Adams' in Boston. After writing "As to Ellen, she is pretty well but I would rather see her a grain more robust before I go away," he went out and Ellen continued the letter.

[41]   [*Philadelphia, March 25*]

Really! —— I have given him leave yea have urged his going away *now* – for he is every whit as much out of his element as at *Concord N.H.* – and (oh tell it not) not a text has he expounded   not a skeleton of a sarmint has he formed   not a sonnet has he perpetuated since he turned his back B ward —— I like Mr & Mrs Furness – I suppose you know them – She is a great deal more beautiful than Sully *has* made or can make her ——

I hope you are good to look in upon the better half of our family at home and now you have our room at that little doll's table so much needed — Philadelphia is the place for room   everything looks as if it asked to be made use of — rooms sufficiently high if your visitor should excell in the tall particular   beds for long and wide – to say nothing of a certain large benevolent look marking the habitants and a liberal bland feeling air that overcomes all suspicions — that gives (makes) one credit for good motives   I wish you could come and see and feel and enjoy —— I dislike N York more than ever and am surprised at the difference in the sensibilities of the fashionables of B & N Y – I wish you would send a kind thought to your brother from me when you can

and believe me I am yours afftly

Ellen

[42]   *[Philadelphia, March 28]*

Dear Aunt Mary –

Through all the journeyings by sea and land   the rains   the equinoctials etc   we have come safely and even pleasantly and have almost resumed the quiet home look & smiles which travellers are so apt to put into their trunks till they arrive at their destined haven —— Mr Turner brought me your letter and it cost me a sigh and a smile – the smile for welcome but the sigh that I was erring from your good counsels and with my strength letting my cheerfulness fail me —— I look back on your visits to us delightedly and strange to tell if I felt an eagerness to see you once I feel a tenfold desire to know you more —— I hope for the sake of keeping up the excitement and being an ever present being in our minds you will not keep your wings always in motion for a flight when you come to see us — but you will call for a while a little window in the dove house your own ——

The winter of sickness & the frosts of *self*ishness will kill this little principle of action if I do not when it begins to be sleepy & benumbed rouse it and exercise it the frozen lake reflects nothing but naked trees and winter scenery – and "the time" may come but the will is gone for the "acts & efforts" —— I had rather – I hope I shall prefer to limp or creep through life casting a glow worm's ray than to live my little day darkly and with my present feelings *wickedly.* When I used to read Dr Doddridge a good deal I longed to feel like the man he speaks of I forget who it was – but he prayed "Oh Lord rather than live without the light of thy countenance and the enjoyment of communion with thee let me die – if I cannot praise thee let me go down to the grave" – He feared no worse misery if he died in darkness and distrust ——

THE LETTERS

I have heard two sermons today   Waldo's "Golden rule" sermon and a sermon by a stranger —— Mr Furness' church is as purely beautiful in *in* and externals as the chastest taste could devise – The mind seems to animate this little band of worshippers after being tossed on a sea of persecution and difficulty they have found a home and a Captain —— When the organ begins the song seems universal and the set choir that is too apt to resemble an aviary is forgotten — the pulpit is merely a raised altar perfectly unornamented and white —— The grass is already richly green in the yard that covers the graves of the departed members —— You would love to worship here I know ——

Waldo talks of leaving me on Wednesday – I do not regret that he is going though his absence will be a thorn to me   But his life is new here – and the ladies parlour or chamber is no place to dust your mind and regulate your soul   and his sermons would not weigh so well as if they were born in his study —— But in May I hope we shall be happy in meeting and I *trust the* elasticity of the bands which bind us farther than the distance of 300 miles   And I wish I could feel a hope of meeting Aunt Mary soon and spending a moment or two with her —— I thank you for your kindness in playing Dr Moody to me and am happy to say from less of a tonic I have found relief – and am very well for me nowadays.

Margaret desires to be remembered to you and so
goodnight says your afft Ellen

This unpublished poem by R.W.E. is to be found at the end of the notebook into which he copied Ellen's verses. It was probably written when he was alone in Boston, having left Ellen and Margaret in Philadelphia.

I am alone. Sad is my solitude.
O thou sweet daughter of God, my angel wife,
Why dost thou leave me thus in the great stranger world
Without one sign or token, one remembrancer
Sent o'er the weary lands that sunder us
To say I greet thee with a beating heart.
Does thy heart beat with mine? does thy blue eye
Ever look northward with desire, O do thy prayers
Remember me when thou hallowest thy maker's name,
Remember him
Who never failed to grace his orison
With thy dear name, believes it acceptable
And prays,   that he may pray for thee –

[43]   [*Philadelphia, April*]

Dear Edward –

I grieve, but I must write with a pencil as we are not people having authority – Many thanks for your wee bit letter and much joy at my increase of facilities for hearing and telling – and joy that you will be here soon —— Philadelphia though beautiful last week is very beautiful now – Here is my mother and there is my sister – and though I fain would say here is Waldo yet I will not breathe so ungratefully —— Do you & William rise at 6 & walk as usual? – You might call at the corner of 11th & Chestnut & find Margaret & myself long gone out and bound either for the banks of Schuylkill or Delaware – There is little of natural beauty I think in the environs of Phil — the little wildflowers look as if Dame Quaker rather than Dame Nature had arranged them and hardly condescend to nodd to Zephyrus as he passes by —— The buildings are chastely beautiful – the U.S. Bank fills the eye — and the fair unruffled Friends gliding unstained and unspotted through the tumult and dust of fashion come like Shadrach Meshach & Abednego through the furnace ——

West's "Christ rejected" I do not admire – too many charcoal strokes about it and in the difficult undertaking of the uncommon expression of the face of Jesus – he failed   I never saw but one that I *wondered* at – by whom I *thought* I should never forget but it is gone now —

1830

I send these letters to you because it is not quite so important whether very soon or a little later they reach B ——

Give my love to William and accept yourself the affection of your sister E ——

Heard yesterday from Waldo – Well but lonely –

This poem is copied into one of R.W.E.'s poetry notebooks, and dated April. It was probably written at the end of April, when he was anxious to go to Philadelphia and bring Ellen back.

To E.T.E. at Philadelphia.

The green grass is bowing,
The morning wind is in it;
'Tis a tune worth thy knowing,
Though it change every minute.

'Tis a tune of the Spring;
Every year plays it over
To the robin on the wing,
And to the pausing lover.

O'er ten thousand, thousand acres,
Goes light the nimble zephyr;
The Flowers – tiny sect of Shakers –
Worship him ever.

Hark to the winning sound!
They summon thee, dearest, –
Saying, 'We have dressed for thee the ground,
Nor yet thou appearest.

'O hasten; 'tis our time,
Ere yet the red Summer
Scorch our delicate prime,
Loved of bee, – the tawny hummer.

'O pride of thy race!
Sad, in sooth, it were to ours,
If our brief tribe miss thy face,
We poor New England flowers.

'Fairest, choose the fairest members
Of our lithe society;
June's glories and September's
Show our love and piety.

'Thou shalt command us all. –
April's cowslip, summer's clover,
To the gentian in the fall,
Blue-eyed pet of blue-eyed lover.

'O come, then, quickly come!
We are budding, we are blowing;
And the wind that we perfume
Sings a tune that's worth the knowing.'

Waldo went to Philadelphia in the middle of May to bring Ellen back. They moved out to Brookline and spent the summer boarding with Mrs. Perry in the old Aspinwall house. Waldo's mother was with them. In September Waldo was back in Boston, and Ellen made a short visit to the Kents in New Hampshire before settling down for the winter in Chardon Street. The following letter is addressed to "William Emerson Esq., Office No 60 Wall St. New York" and postmarked "New York Aug 2". William endorsed it "Ellen & Waldo Emerson July 30/30." The date line is in R.W.E.'s hand.

[44] *30 July Brookline*

W. & E.

And shall I dare to write to my brothers in this cold drizzle of a storm – lest my thoughts should catch the indigo tinge and be a faggot of woes — I would not but for the hope that ere the travelled sheet arrives a bright sun and a summer air will be counteracters of its influence and reflect a brightness on the pages — but here I talk as if I were going to write a book to you when I shall only say how do ye and Good bye —— I hear you like Clarence – well I find everybody inclined to – but I cant – It seems to me the characters in general are like all in novels – saving the heroine who is as perfectly unatural as a spirit and full of *supernaturality* – I was just thinking if I chanced to know Miss S I might admire but I think again it is of her book alone that I speak and my likes and dislikes are as it is the more just for being unbiassed ——

Our Mother sits by me reading it and by her un-

1830

broken attention has found it at least very attractive – looking a wee bit paler & thinner than usual on account of a little indisposition – but as calm & serene as a summer sky – They tell of Time's irresistible finger – in truth a chain seems to have been thrown around him as he approached and affliction has only mellowed not darkened the picture – I would there were more such beautiful instances of virtue's embalming power how few would shrink and fear to count the summers that are on them

    We sigh not when the sun his course fulfilled
    His glorious course rejoicing earth and sky
    In the soft evening when the winds are stilled
    Sinks where the islands of refreshment lie — says Bryant so prettily ——

We hear from Charles of his realized anticipation – and continued love — though disappointed of one of his companions But I'll say Good bye now for Waldo will write you a word —— your sister afftly
                                              Ellen ——

The rest of the letter is written by R.W.E.; see Rusk, *Letters*, p. 306.

THE LETTERS

This unfinished letter was folded and tucked into one of Ellen's notebooks. It apparently dates from the autumn of 1830, after Ellen, Waldo, and Waldo's mother had moved back into Boston from Brookline. The "Ellen" addressed might have been a slightly younger cousin, Aunt Washburn's daughter.

[45] [*Autumn, 1830*]

My dear Ellen —

Here sit I in my own little domicile & *realize* that I am Mrs Emerson to the full for Betsy & Nancy and Martin must have their daily & nightly tasks allotted – and Mr Such a one with his wife are in town and they must come to tea tomorrow – no cake – bless me how many eggs? how much sugar? and there are those brasses and the spare chamber bed must be attended — only imagine the careless, one eyed skittish Ellen Tucker in this situation & send her a little fairy Order to tap with her wand upon the household duds and ease me of my woe —— Do I alarm you? Verily I am happier than it often falleth to the lot of mortals to be and am thrice happy to be able to offer you chamber – 3 if so many you choose to occupy and the hearty welcome of 3 united hearts namely R W & E T & Mother — come if you set your face Boston wardly directly to Chardon St for we keep the same house that last winter we borrowed – I shall expect you very confidently —— And you – what a grand correspondent you make – I did not hurry to answer the letter that you warned me was the last   How seldom do we do a good action disinterestedly   Have you learned

1830

the Trojans out? and what of French Parlez vous Français? Ecrivez vous Français? Entendez vous la langue Française?

The next letter is addressed in R.W.E.'s handwriting to "Edward B. Emerson Esq. Care of Mr. Geo. Barnard Santa Croix." It is endorsed in Edward's writing "R.W. & Ell. L. Emerson 24 Decr 1830" The date at the head of the letter is in R.W.E.'s writing.

[46]   *Boston   24 Dec 1830*

Dear Edward

Ere this you are breathing beautiful balm and Old Winter has just in good earnest breathed hard upon us – thermometer at 6, snow, wind, long icicles   blue noses and sad looking invalids — you're a king and may hug yourself for your timely retreat — Pray speak kindly to the Santa Cruzians of all your kith & kin and pick out a pretty spot for Waldo & wife to live – for such golden dreams in spite of 2d church and blk gown Bostonians? Concordians   do I indulge   But some day   tut! all inconvenience will meet you like Bishop Bruno or Hatto's rats wherever you go – Cold winds and changes here   scorpions & debilities there —— The latter I urge are not so soul annoying as the former – One is a slow, uncertain death or an ill-spent life   the other a quick and sure remedy or a certain an not agreeable but more preferable death —— You perhaps are so new to & transient in the invalid table that you will never understand me when I speak so strongly

Aunt Mary has appeared in our home an instant but the whole was like a dream – She seems not of the earthly nor altogether of the heavenly – to be wondered at and in some sort admired – She has gone with Charles to Concord where she means if it seemeth her good after a trial to pass the coming winter ——

The rest of the letter is written by R.W.E.; see Rusk, *Letters* p. 314.

[47] *[Undated]*

Dear Aunt Hubbard

How very neglectful you must have supposed me & ungrateful for your kindness in not acknowledging the reciept of that medicine which altho' it failed to cure afforded me a temporary relief —— Paulina went off very unexpectedly and since her departure I have been very unwell myself and Mother has been suffering from the great enemy of our family lung complaints – she has raised some blood and looks pale & thin I am so anxious – I cannot tell you how anxious – But her spirits are very good and every fair day she rides out – & seems delighted that she is with her children – I have no doubt if she goes with M & myself to Philadelphia but she will be much better and there is little immediate danger to apprehend ——

I hope you are all well but am almost afraid to ask for the variableness and dampness of the weather has been such that strong constitutions have been sorely tried —— I suppose this winter will not bring you unless we have some very tempting sleighing and then if you would hop into a sleigh with Uncle and a bundle of cousins you would make us very happy —— Give my love to Uncle P & the 2 Hs and kiss the little dear cousins all for me –

    Your afft niece
    Ellen T. Emerson

[48]   [*January 1831*]

Dear Aunt Mary

 Even now am I as stupid & unlovely as when you were here. Waldo has gone to preach and Mother to hear and I am left to pout it out or perchance to find relief in some magical leaf of poetry or musick note or thread of thought —— I thank you for praying for Waldo such good prayers – and to send me some spirits – I verily need them as much as he for tho' my task be less my lack is more – I don't write to you because I hate to write bad when I can write better or have written better but it is in vain to attempt to tell how dry & arid my soul is — and to recieve in answer you are not expected or you are not made to do – I do – but it is as one moulding the air ——

 I like Waldo's sermon to night and my views of benevolence – or motives for benevolence – are clearer – but the new year's eve was indeed a failure (he says) and the year went out – but its wing was hardly heard it fluttered and fluttered and crept at last ——

 My Mother has raised blood, a drop of vermeil

should be the family coat of arms   I tell her it seems to be a small life insurance but sigh to see her beginning again a siege of blistering, soaking —— Margaret is well and still dreams on – tho' occasionally starting in slumber – speaks of you – I wish you could come again and finish your visit   you did not disturb me and I now begin to count weeks of my stay North   Phila in 6 weeks —— You shall have my chamber and my pills —— Mother has been looking for a gown for you but how can you expect to be clothed in scarlet or crimson without paying for it —— However you shant have a black as the shawl turned out to be –

Please to remember me to Grandfather most affectionately and respectfully and bid him gladden us once more with his presence — we will not urge him against his weal (in body or mind) to stay —— Charles & Mother & Waldo are well and regret your absence often

Goodnight dear Aunt Mary
— says Ellen T E ——

This goodnight message is apparently the last of Ellen's letters.

Epilogue

At the end of January 1831, Waldo wrote to Edward and William that his poor Ellen had been sick. Charles kept in touch with Aunt Mary and reported on February 4th that he did not think she could live but a very short time. "It was not till this morning," he wrote, "I felt as if I was to part from her. God be merciful to her husband." On February 6th he wrote again: "Ellen is still with us – tho' her spirit seems winged for its flight. She spoke this afternoon very sweetly of her readiness to die – that she told you she should not probably live through the winter – tho' she did not know that she should have been called so soon – She saw no reason why her friends should be distressed – it was better she should go first, & prepare the way – She asked Waldo, if he had strength, to read her a few verses of scripture – and he read a portion of the XIVth chapter of John —— Waldo is bowed down under the affliction, yet he says 'tis like seeing an angel go to Heaven. Her mother has been able to be with her these last two or three days & that is a very great satisfaction to them both. Margaret is with her constantly."

On February 8th Waldo wrote to Aunt Mary: "My angel is gone to heaven this morning & I am alone in the world & strangely happy. Her lungs shall no more be torn nor her head scalded by her blood nor her

EPILOGUE

whole life suffer from the warfare between the force & delicacy of her soul & the weakness of her frame. I said this morn & I do not know but it is true that I have never known a person in the world in whose separate existence as a soul I could so readily & fully believe & she is present with me now beaming joyfully upon me, in her deliverance & the entireness of her love for your poor nephew. I see it plainly that things & duties will look coarse & vulgar enough to me when I find the romance of her presence (& romance is a beggarly word) withdrawn from them all. But now the fulness of joy occasioned by things said by her in the last week & by this eternal deliverance is in my heart."

Ellen was buried near her father in Roxbury. The young minister mourned deeply. His brothers report his stunned and depressed condition to each other in letters. He wrote elegies and laments for Ellen in his journal. Her name recurs many times for many years. He left the church, and became the well-known lecturer, the poet, the essayist, the Sage of Concord. His second marriage was a happy one; in Lydia Jackson of Plymouth he found an intelligent and loving companion. But he had written that "there is one birth, one baptism, and one first love."

Emerson has left us a great deal, but there is little left of her who in letters and journals was always synonymous with light and flowers, love and beauty – the "sweet singer, sainted wife," the "enchanting friend," who "outshone all beauty," who shed a "tender and

EPILOGUE

immortal light." An unflattering miniature, four partially filled notebooks, and these letters are the actual relics that remain. The influence of her life on Ralph Waldo Emerson, however, is a legacy whose importance is hard to overestimate. Her memory retained its vividness for him. He was remembering her eight years later, shortly before the birth of the daughter who was to carry on her name, and he wrote: "Ellen was never alone. I could not imagine her poor and solitary. She was like a tree in flower, so much soft, budding, and informing beauty was society for itself, and she taught the eye that beheld her, why Beauty was ever painted with loves and graces attending her steps."

In R.W.E.'s journal for 1831, following his description of Ellen's death, is a series of poems, hastily written, mostly unfinished, about Ellen, and about death. Two of these follow. The first one is the earliest of the group, dated February 15.

    Dost thou not hear me   Ellen
    Is thy ear deaf to me
    Is thy radiant eye
    Dark that it cannot see

    In yonder ground thy limbs are laid
    Under the snow
    And earth has no spot so dear above
    As that below

    And there I know the heart is still
    And the eye is shut and the ear is dull

    But the spirit that dwelt in mine,
    The spirit wherein mine dwelt
    The soul of Ellen, the thought divine
    From God that came – for all that felt

    Does it not know me now
    Does it not share my thought?
    Is it prisoned from Waldo's prayer
    Is its glowing love forgot?

Dust unto dust! and shall no more be said,
Ellen, for thee, and shall a common fate
Blend thy last hour with the last hours of all?
Of thee, my wife, my undefiled, my dear?
The muse thy living beauty could inspire
Shall spare one verse to strew thy urn
Or be forever silent.   Ellen is dead,
She who outshone all beauty, yet knew not
That she was beautiful, she who was fair
After another mould than flesh and blood.
Her beauty was of God. The maker's hand
Yet rested on its work,
And cast an atmosphere of sanctity
Around her steps that pleased old age and youth;
Yea, that not won the eye, but did persuade
The soul by realizing human hopes,
Teaching that faith and love were not a dream
Teaching that purity had yet a shrine,
And that the innocent and affectionate thoughts
That harbour in the bosom of a child
Might live embodied in a riper form,
And dwell with wisdom never bought by sin.
Blessed, sweet singer, were the ears that heard;
To her the eye that saw bare witness –
The holy light of her eye did prophesy
The impatient heaven that called her hence.

PART THREE

POEMS AND NOTEBOOKS

✞

THE POEMS

Ralph Waldo Emerson wrote in his journal in 1847, "Ellen Tucker's poetry was very sweet, and on the way to all high merits and yet as easy as breathing to her who wrote it." He copied eighteen of her poems into a small notebook labeled "Ellen's Verses." Many of these exist only in his copy, nowhere in her handwriting. He did not arrange them in chronological order, and it is difficult to ascertain when some of them were written. There are in existence four notebooks of hers, two of which contain original verses mostly written quite early. Only one poem can be dated exactly — "Go my lamb," which in Emerson's collection is given the title "To her lamb which was killed on the occasion of producing a collation for Lafayette in 1825." She was thirteen or fourteen at the time. This was the year of her brother George's death; her sister Mary had died earlier. The poems of this period are mostly about falling leaves, dying flowers, changing seasons, and are deeply tinged with melancholy.

A sort of chronological order has been followed in the following selections. The "pale Violet" refers to Mary, and "Weave, weave," was presumably inspired by George's death. The love poems can be placed in 1829. The last fragments appear in her notebook, but were not copied by Emerson. Nor did he copy a single line in pencil near the end that might have been the beginning of her last poem to him:

"Thy love hath been like morning's dawn" —

THE VIOLET

Why lingerest thou, pale Violet, to see the dying year
Are autumn blasts fit music for thee, fragile one, to hear;
Will thy clear blue eye upwards bent still keep its chastened glow
Still tearless lift its slender form above the wintry snow?

Why wilt thou live when none around reflect thy pensive ray
Thou bloomest here a lonely thing in the clear autumn day
The tall green trees that shelter thee their last gay dress put on
There will be nought to shelter thee when their sweet leaves are gone.

Oh violet, like thee how blest could I lie down and die,
When summer light is fading, and autumn breezes sigh,
When winter reigned I'd close my eye, but wake with bursting spring
And live with living Nature, a pure rejoicing thing.

I had a sister once who seemed just like a violet,
Her morning sun shone bright, and calmly purely set;
When the violets were in their shrouds and summer in its pride
She laid her hopes at rest, and in the years rich beauty died.

TO HER LAMB,
which was killed on the occasion of providing a collation for Lafayette, 1825.

Go, my lamb, though drop by drop
Half my heart will bleed for thee –
Go – for mercy do not stop –
Go ere love shall conquer me.

Memories do not use your power,
Ye are tender, bright and dear,
Love will bleed for one sweet flower,
Tears begone – intrude not here.

Go, my lamb – a sacrifice
Greater far was made for me,
Purer, whiter was the gift
Loss more sad than thine can be.

Loss it seemed to all below
But at last how great the gain,
Pearls in all the streams that flow
From the lamb for me was slain

– Go   my lamb –

Weave – weave the low funereal melody
Hang o'er this cold & lonely stone a wreath
Of rue & yew & cypress melancholy
Low his fair innocence & manly pride
And youthful frolick – still & deathlike here.
The moon with eye unaltered now looks down
But when awhile ago the vault did yawn
For its last victim – then she hid her face
And in the midnight watches many tell
She was not where she should be.
Sweep sighing o'er, the damp airs of the night,
Winter! thy winding sheet send floating down.
Coldness & dark & damp befit this grave
The grave of many a young unripened heart.

I will not stay on earth   Waldo
Unless thy love is mine
When all that gave it birth   my love
And beauty must decline

No   let me when thine eye on me
Falls coldly as on all
To the home that ever will be free
And ope to Misery's call

Sweeter the green sod for my bones
The black earth for my head
The wind,   than thy cold altered tones
Whence all of love had fled.

Love scatters oil
On Life's dark Sea
Sweetens its toil
Our helmsman he

Around him hover
Odorous clouds
Under this cover
His arrows he shrouds.

The cloud was around me
I knew not why
Such sweetness crowned me
While time shot by.

No pain was within
But calm delight
Like a world without sin
Or a day without night.

The shafts of the god
Were tipped with down
For they drew no blood
And knit no frown.

I knew not of them
Till Cupid laughed loud
And saying   you're caught
Flew off in the cloud.

Oh   then I awoke
And I lived but to sigh
I've done with grief now
I shan't tell why.

Thou left'st thy ninety-nine to seek
Thy loved & cherished one
Fear painted wind & tempest bleak
Thy ewe lamb sick & lone.

Ah   few who seek as quickly find
Few lost ones smile again
Few save the strained & opening link
From breaking up the chain.

And lost at last – when thy sad step
On earth in vain may stray
When from thy bosom's temporal shield
God calls his own away

Still shalt thou hold thy parted one
In blest security
When we in our great Shepherd's fold
Two lambs together lie.

Dear love, our Father in the sky
And 'tis not ours to question why
Decrees that days & months divide
Louisa from her Waldo's side.

Oh, sparkling health, the peasant's prize,
Will surely bless the sacrifice
And I shall buy with seas of tears
A score or two of rosy years.

Oh gold   how dim your yellow eye
Oh pomp   how rusty you become
When weighed with labor's roseate dye
The healthy busy humble home.

Love feels the blight of Sickness' touch
And shrinks beneath her selfish chill
Old Time then hobbles with a crutch
And clouds the once blue heavens fill.

But why so sad? And if I'm sold
To the pale maid – while here I move
Soon my thin years on earth are told
And I shall breathe the air of love.

I chided the moon, she was icy cold –
The stars were coquettes too splendidly drest
Found fault with the gorgeous hues of gold
That fringe the sky at the hour of rest.

But I bless the stars as they twinkle now
And feel a kindlier heat for the moon
Although she is cold as she kisses my brow
And watcheth my vigil at night's still noon.

They tell me mine eye hath ceased to roam
Like a midnight spirit seeking rest
But quietly beams as if sure of a home
In the depths of a pure and faithful breast.

It hath found a home & is blest indeed
My spirit hath folded her waving wing
And lifts herself up like a trusting reed
A happier holier purer thing.

When we're angels in heaven
Dont raving mad be
If without notice given
I stay out to tea.

For what e'er sister angel
My presence may honour
I think you may as well
Place dependance upon her.

I shan't keep a carriage
My wings will be strong
And our earthly marriage
Will be vain as a song.

I therefore shall use them
As I may see fit
And tea out and dine out
Nor mind you a bit.

'Tis well, like weary wandering dove,
Our restless foot returns
From vain pursuit of earthly love
To where God's altar burns.

E'en if grim death or sickness send
No dart to crush our pride;
If the grave yawn not for a friend
Nor poverty abide;

E'en in the rose, that beauteous thing,
There lurks an anguish fell;
Our friend will turn in hate to sting
For loving him too well.

To the South Wind.

O come not now to lure
Me back to earth again
That moment I was sure
I felt the latest pain.

And yet ye're heaven's messenger
And bear soft words to me;
But breathe not yet, but wait until
My spirit is set free.

Then whisper round my grave
The tale of my release –

How true! each hours researches prove
Our Father's tenderness and love
Green earth, deep sea, the peopled air
Lift up their voices and declare

And more than mines of buried ore
Than in hid treasures how much more
Do I his love and favor see
In making thee   my love   for me.

As nature's gems lie hid in night
Till art descends with welcome light
Or as when found they rayless lie
Till she her skillful influence ply

So I – unless God's guiding love
Had brought thee to me from above
Might now have lived but half an one
A moving world without a sun

We have within our souls "the tree
Of glorious immortality
3 branches point like spires above
Fair virtue, intellect, & love" —

I am the grave's,   its seal is set upon me
It's chalky white & startling vermeil red
I am the grave's   with death cold hand it warns me
My home is never here   & my weak ease
I'm warned to leave –

And Hope, sweet bird & kind, at last has flown
And of her beauty scarce a trace is found
Save a slight tinge where her last splendour shone
And there a golden feather quivering on the ground –
Just bright enough to cheat the eager eye
Just strong enough temptation for a lie

THE NOTEBOOKS

Ellen's earliest notebook contains twenty-three pages of poetry copied out in a very formal and elegant handwriting, as though for exercise in penmanship. There are nineteen poems, of which three are by Mrs Hemans — "The Hour of Death," "To a dead Child," and "Farewell to a dead Youth." L.E.L. (Letitia Elizabeth Landon) is represented by two very mournful poems. The other authors are not identified but their tone is equally gloomy. These are some of the first lines: "Weep not, though lonely and wild be thy path," "True, all we know must die," "So forget me, why should sorrow, o'er that brow a shadow fling," "He sleeps, the infant sufferer sleeps." A few poems about stars, friends, and love are somewhat more cheerful. The last two bits of poetry have the following endings:

>Hopes like meteors that shine and depart,
>An early grave and a broken ♡

and

>Of love that passed like the lava wave,
>Of a broken heart and an early grave –

Then written in an extremely dashing and untidy manner across the last page comes the outburst "Oh, Miss Landon, a broken ♡ and an early grave ——." This must have been penned after the end of the last class.

The second notebook begins with the address "Londonderry," which is followed by the poem on

Miss Grant (see note, Letter 11); it must have been used by Ellen while at school. References to George's death place the date in 1825. There is a poem about her father, and one to her mother which begins:

> I am a feeble reed – yet as my sun matures
> And thine declinest – Mother lean on me
> Take thou my willing arm for thy support
> I'll guide thy tottering steps as age creeps on
> And smooth before thee thy remaining way.

Ellen must have been fourteen years old at this time. The rest of the notebook contains many unfinished verses; pages of blank verse about life, autumn and winter, morning and night, etc.; a ballad-like poem beginning "Lady, your cheek is vermeiled like a flower," verses to a robin in the wood; and several pages of moralizing on various subjects — "There is not a soul in the wide world but hath felt at some time a respect for God," and so forth. The last poem is about falling leaves, and ends:

> I would not be a leaf to live in one
> Short summer's sun one heavenly day,
> Then loosened softly from my parent stem
> To flutter darkly on the barren earth,
> No spot beyond – my last – my only home.

The only other notebook is George's journal, which must have been returned to the family after his death in Paris, and which was taken over by Ellen. There are few clues to the dates of composition.

Waldo's name does not appear till well past the middle of this small book.

Ellen starts writing on a Sunday in October: "O this day-dreaming with my eyes open what a foe it is to me – to devotional feeling and nearness to God – I seem to be dead to all – to everything – to have no mind – for I can recall no image that has occupied me no land that has enchanted me – when oh when shall I have these truant affections of mine in leading strings –" There are indications that she was sick part of the time she was using this notebook. Her poem on the South Wind indicates illness, and is preceded by this bit of prose: "The sweet south wind has been playing about us all day – I dread it – it excites me strongly – and I thought it told of war & blood today —— It smelt too of melted snow – and swept over the altered cheek of nature in sweet funereal melodies – Farewell Farewell It fans dying nature and her eye kindles in death brightly like the breeze bringing new life to gasping consumptives —"

As in the earlier book there are obscure and melancholy verses, often left unfinished, and more thoughts on moral and religious subjects, such as the following: "Little Fido sat with his master in an old decaying summer house while he slept – Fido heard a noise, feels the crumbles of plastering come down on his head – Instinct says danger is near – Fido tries in every way to awake his master in vain – at last he hops up and bites his little finger and thus preserves his life – happy we if we are spared a little Fido to awake our slumbering consciences – who spare us not the pain present – to enable us to escape future destruction – Fido awake in me!"

The page preceding the first mention of Waldo's name, in the verses "I will not stay on earth, Waldo," contains these comments on her affections: "Riding at the circus for days the restrained canter of some of the horses I cannot but compare to my affections – They can canter smoothly gratefully and strong, only give them room enough but curb them and their strength shows itself in certain uneasy motions disagreeable very to the rider who is inclined to doubt the ability of the horse – So my affecs – being often curbed for want of room they do render me disagreeable to others and vastly uncomfortable myself —"

Waldo is not mentioned again, but one of his poems ("And do I waste my time") is tucked into the book, and also her poem "Love scatters oil." On the same sheet with this are some small sketches, and the names "R. W. Emerson" and "E. L. Tucker" bracketed together. On the other side of the sheet she wrote: "What shall I do? What shall I do? Wednesday I turn my back to the light and farewell to ye — real comforts — I have naught but your memories to comfort me — I say they are not idle words – these that lovers repeat – 'Je vous aime' – it is their world – Oh what insulated beings it makes us – we centre all our thoughts in one spot – in the eyes in the smile the voice of a being and this being saith 'go' & we go & 'do this' & we do it – but stronger still 'come' and we come and are happy ——

I believe God loves to see two of his creatures love each other dearly——" This was probably written in August 1829 when Waldo had just left for Boston, as she uses the word "insulated" in two letters to him at this time.

It seems probable that she kept other journals, and destroyed them. In one of the last letters before their marriage (number 34) she warned Waldo that "the journals are dangerously sick . . . be not downcast if they have departed this life ere you arrive and the beautiful ashes be all that is left . . . I prefer to have no record so distinct of the past."

One other small book exists, but its contents are hard to identify or classify. It is an album with a printed title-page dated New Haven 1826. It could have been a present to Ellen from her stepfather, Colonel Kent, who was invited to write the first poem in it. The poem is dated "Decr 1826" and signed "Dad." It begins:

> You ask me to inscribe a verse
> And offer this fair page,
> But can you look for "words which burn"
> Amidst the *frosts of age*?
>
> No, but *affection* prompts the wish
> Some token to retain,
> If favored by events in life
> Remembrance may remain.

Then take these lines my lovely child
Parental fondness pens
He gives them you at your request,
With you their value ends.

Except for four poems near the end which appear to be in Ellen's early handwriting, the nineteen poems which follow are apparently original verses in several different handwritings, of little poetic value. Several are addressed to Ellen by name, and all are full of sentiment and gentle melancholy. The following effort is typical:

> As in the clear unruffled stream
> The trees that shade its bank we see,
> When o'er this page thy eye shall beam
> May in thy heart my image be.
> And as the waters onward stray
> Each wave reflects its banks anew,
> May I, when years have roll'd away,
> Still live, in memory, for you.

A long one entitled "Dreamings" was written on June tenth, and the year must have been 1827 or 1828. In her letters to Waldo Ellen refers to earlier suitors and love letters, but the identity of the authors of these poems can probably not be ascertained.

The poems that seem to be in Ellen's early handwriting are gentle and sentimental. One begins, "I've been to take a fond leave-taking look," describes a number of favorite places, and ends: "Friends! farewell – farewell – ". Another is in the same vein, about memories of earlier days and those who have left but return in visions.

It seems probable that Ellen kept this anthology of verses with her, and that Waldo, seeing it after their engagement and finding many blank pages in it, wrote briefly in it also. He wrote her name on the fly leaf. Further along he wrote: " 'L'Amitié est l'Amour sans ailes,' et mon affection, ma belle reine, est une amitié amoureuse, puisqu'elle a tout le feu de l'amour, mais elle n'a point d'ailes; pas une plume. Oh Ellen, elle ne peut pas mouvoir: c'est un rocher. ——— " He used one more page, and wrote:

"Voltaire's inscription upon the statue of Cupid.
Qui que tu sois, voici ton maitre,
Il l'est, le fut, ou le dois etre."

"The moon being clouded presently is missed
But little stars may hide them when they list."

Tucked into the album are scraps of paper, and pressed leaves and flower petals. A charming small water-color profile is also there with the notation "Mrs Washburn GWT" — a picture of Aunt Washburn by her nephew George Tucker. One small sliver of cardboard has written on it,
"Waldo   I love you   Ellen."

NOTES

NOTES ON THE TEXT

INDEX

Notes

Page 2

The quotations from R.W.E.'s letters here and elsewhere are taken from Ralph L. Rusk, *The Letters of Ralph Waldo Emerson* (New York: Columbia University Press, 1939). Letters written by Charles, Edward, William, and Mary Moody Emerson have not been published. They are the property of the R.W.E. Memorial Association, and are in the Houghton Library of Harvard University.

Bezaleel Tucker was born in 1771, and was the third son of Nathaniel and Hannah Tucker of Middleboro, Massachusetts. There were ten other children — Andrew, Cyrus, Salmon, Boadicea, Alanson, Lucy, Zelotes, Nathaniel, Serena, and Paulina. Bezaleel (usually called Beza) owned a ropewalk in Boston, and lived in the Sumner mansion on the Dedham turnpike in Roxbury until his death in 1820.

William Austin Kent had come to Concord, New Hampshire, from Charlestown, Massachusetts, in 1789, at the age of twenty-four. He had set up a shop, and had married Charlotte Mellen. Within a few years he seems to have become one of the active and leading citizens. The list of his interests and activities is very long. In 1795 he was one of a group granted a charter for a toll bridge over the Merrimac. In 1802 he was on a committee to enlarge the meeting house, and in 1806 he was connected with the first incorporated bank. A little later he gave land so that the present State Street could be laid out, moderated the town meeting, and was on the committee to build the State House. He was a volunteer in the War of 1812. In 1826 he became active in church affairs, and helped form the new Unitarian Society which invited Ralph Waldo Emerson to come and preach. He was a director of the

NOTES

Concord "Lower" Bank for many years, and was on the board of an insurance company and of a trading company which ran boats on the Merrimac River and the Middlesex Canal between Concord and Boston. He must have been socially gifted and able, since it was at his house that President Monroe was entertained in 1817 and the Marquis of Lafayette in 1825. Daniel Webster visited frequently. Apparently Colonel Kent was a quiet man, who did not talk much, but when he did, his words were witty and to the point. Two of his sons, William and George, had houses in Concord and were also active in town affairs.

Page 6

Mary Moody Emerson, younger sister of Waldo's father William, frequently boarded with her sister-in-law Ruth after her brother's death in 1811, and helped to supervise the boys' education. E.W.Emerson (*Emerson in Concord*) says: "It would be hard to overestimate the effect upon these minds of this same proud, pious, eccentric, exacting, inspiring Aunt Mary Moody Emerson." Waldo was her favorite, and the correspondence between them which began in 1813 when he was nine continued till her death fifty years later. His interesting article about her appears in *Letters and Biographical Sketches*. No young person, he says, "could have met her without remembering her with interest, and learning something of value. Scorn trifles, lift your eyes: do what you are afraid to do: sublimity of character must come from sublimity of motive: these were the lessons which were urged with vivacity in ever new language." Unfortunately Emerson's letters to her at this time are missing, but a fragment of one written January 6, 1829, is quoted in his journal. He describes his and his brothers' state of well-being at the moment, and continues, "Now I add to all this felicity a particular felicity which makes my own glass very much larger and fuller . . . I should be glad, dear Aunt, that you, who are my oldest friend, would give me some of your meditations upon these new leaves of my for-

NOTES

tune." Waldo and Ellen must have wondered how Aunt Mary would feel about their marriage. She became very fond of Ellen, curls and all, and one of Ellen's last letters to her is endorsed' "Dear gone Ellen's."

Page 11

    Letter 1. Postmarked: Concord N.H. Dec. 29; begun Sunday, December 28, 1828, and completed on Monday, December 29.

Page 13

    "Charles 5th": William Robertson's *History of the Reign of the Emperor Charles V,* first published in 1769.

Page 14

    One can only guess that John Williams had been one of Ellen's beaux. The word "little" occurs before a name several times in her letters and may be a reference to R.W.E.'s height compared to that of the other men she had known.

    "Pres Kirkland": John Thornton Kirkland, president of Harvard University from 1810 to 1828.

Page 15

    Miss Sparhawk was probably Elizabeth, daughter of the Samuel Sparhawk who had been associated with Colonel Kent in various town activities. Mr. Sparhawk and Colonel Kent were both active politically in the 1828 presidential campaign as Adams, or National, Republicans.

    "Brother Edward": Edward Kent, Colonel Kent's fourth son. He and R.W.E. were both members of the class of 1821 at Harvard.

    Forget me not. The Token. The Talisman. These are the names of gift-books, or annuals, small books containing poetry and prose. The *Forget me not* was published in London and Philadelphia in 1828, and R.W.E. had given a copy to Ellen. *The Token, a Christmas and New Years Present,* was published in Boston in 1828, and *The Talisman* in New York in 1827 and 1828.

NOTES

"Ah fate cannot etc" is probably a reference to a poem called "Fame," written by R.W.E. in 1824, which begins:

> Ah Fate, cannot a man
> Be wise without a beard?
> East, West, from Beer to Dan,
> Say, was it ever heard
> That wisdom might in youth be gotten
> Or wit be ripe before 'twas rotten?

Page 16

"To Ellen." This first poem obviously belongs to the time of their engagement, but could have been written either at the end of December 1828 or in January 1829. It occurs in R.W.E.'s journal, Houghton 15.

Page 18

Letter 2. Postmarked: Worcester Ms. May 1; written Thursday, April 30, 1829.

Page 19

"ken." Ellen's use of Scotch dialect — "ken," "gang to rest," "fash yourself," etc. — must be the result of her reading of ballads, Scott's *Border Minstrelsy* and other collections. These ballads were favorites of R.W.E. and many were later included in his collection *Parnassus*. The Waverley Novels which contain Scotch dialect may also have influenced her diction.

Page 20

"The airy frostwork" refers to hopes of good health that melted away like frost when Ellen was sick the preceding January after her family had moved to Boston. See note to Letter 9.

Dr. James Jackson was a Boston physician, a professor at Harvard. Later references indicate that he was Ellen's doctor, and that R.W.E. frequently consulted him about her health. The reference to the house in the apple tree is obscure.

"departed Ware" was the Reverend Henry Ware, who had preceded R.W.E. at the Second Church in Boston.

NOTES

Page 21

"Grampa," both here and in later letters, is presumably a teasing comment on the eight years difference in their ages.

"P & M" were Ellen's two older sisters, Paulina and Margaret.

Letter 3. Postmarked: Hartford Ct. May 4

"Election." According to Van Dusen's *Connecticut* (New York, 1961), "Jackson supporters, taking the title 'Democrats' decided to run candidates in the April 1829 state elections, but the Republicans won easily."

Page 22

"I am content with what I have . . ." is quoted from the shepherd boy's song in Bunyan's *Pilgrim's Progress*:

I am content with what I have,
Little be it or much;
And, Lord, contentment still I crave,
Because thou savest such.

Page 23

"The Land o' the Leal," by Lady Caroline Nairn, ends as follows:

Now fare ye well, my ain Jean!
This world's care is vain, Jean!
We'll meet, and aye be fain
  In the Land o' the Leal.

The "red morroco case" contained the miniature of Ellen, painted by Miss Sarah Goodridge, which is mentioned in a letter from R.W.E. to William, April 10th, 1829. R.W.E. wrote: "Ellen is pretty well. Miss Goodridge visited her today for the last time to finish her miniature wherewith I shall shortly be enriched." This miniature was reproduced in the Houghton Mifflin *Journals* (1909). Since then it has disappeared, and the illustration on plate 2 in this book is taken from an old photograph owned by the Emerson family. The

NOTES

Concord (Massachusetts) Antiquarian Society was given in 1936 a miniature of Ellen, said to have been painted by Miss Caroline Schetky. A comparison between the photograph and this miniature indicates that the latter may be a copy of the original. The photograph shows more of the pattern on the red shawl, and the shawl hangs in a more natural manner. The hair also seems less stiff. It is possible that Miss Schetky copied the Goodridge miniature for one of Ellen's relatives or friends. On the other hand, Ellen's request to R.W.E. to bring with him when he comes in June "the first edition of the Morocco case by Miss Goodrich" suggests that Miss Goodridge herself painted two versions of the miniature. Two small lockets, less than one inch square, showing Ellen's face, were also copied. One of these is owned by the Emerson family, the other by the Concord Antiquarian Society.

R.W.E.'s miniature, painted between January and April 1829, was also by Miss Goodridge. The miniature has disappeared and the illustration on plate 3 is reproduced from a small photograph owned by the R.W.E. Memorial Association. This miniature is described by F. S. Sanborn ("Portraits of Emerson," New England Magazine, December 1896), with the comment that "neither Mrs. Emerson nor the children recalled the period when it was a good likeness, if ever it can have been." This assertion contradicts a note on the back of the photograph in E. W. Forbes's handwriting: "Mother (Edith Emerson Forbes) says that Grandmother liked it and said it was perfect of him at the time."

Page 25

"And do I waste my time . . ." This poem is written on a small piece of paper tucked into "George's notebook," Houghton 158.

Page 26

Letter 4. Postmarked: Hartford Ct. May 6; written on Tuesday and Wednesday, May 5 and 6, 1829.

NOTES

"Herbert's herb for expression" is a reference to the sixth verse of George Herbert's poem *Providence*:

> Who hath the virtue to express the rare
> And common virtues both of herbs and stones?
> Is there an herb for that? O that thy care
> Would show a root that gives expressions!

Page 27
The "Gov" was Gideon Tomlinson, Republican governor of Connecticut from 1827 to 1831.

"Morgan's" was an inn, the "good quarters" mentioned in the letter of May 4, where Colonel Kent usually stayed in Hartford.

Page 29
R.W.E.'s aunt, Hannah Haskins Kast, lived in Hartford, and "the cousins" were doubtless her daughter Sally and Sally's husband George Shepard.

Letter 5. "Ellinelli's song" is adapted from a popular song by Charles E. Horn called "I've been roaming." It begins:

> I've been roaming, I've been roaming,
> Where the meadow dew is sweet,
> And I'm coming, and I'm coming,
> With its pearls upon my feet.

Page 30
Where Ellen mentions that R.W.E. will say that she "spatters ink about," there are several large splashes of ink across the upper corner of the sheet.

Page 31
Letter 6. Postmarked: Concord N.H. May 22. In addition to the endorsement indicated at the head of the letter, R.W.E. wrote below the message "Recd May 23, 1829"

Letter 7. Postmarked: Concord N.H. May 25; written on May 23.

NOTES

Mr. and Mrs. Abiel Chandler kept a boarding-house in Boston on Cross Street, where the Kents had apparently stayed. They had left some of their things there to be picked up later, or had forgotten something.

Letter 8. Postmarked: Concord N.H. May 25. The letter was begun on Sunday May 24, and finished Monday.

Page 32

Ellen's mention of the "6 days" since they parted indicates that the Kents and Ellen returned from the Worcester and Hartford trip and spent four or five days in Boston before moving back to Concord for the summer, on May 19, according to the letter of May 12.

In the *History of Concord N.H.* (Concord, 1903) "Paradise" is described as a region north of the town beyond Woods Brook, so named because of its beautiful scenery, with a grove of trees, and views of the Merrimac to the east.

"Mr Thomas." In 1827, a group of Unitarians of whom Colonel Kent was one had separated from the old North Church, and had formed the Second Congregational Society of Concord. Moses G. Thomas was ordained in 1828 as its first minister.

Page 33

"Mrs Lyman." Anne Robbins Lyman was the wife of Judge Joseph Lyman of Northhampton, Massachusetts. R.W.E. had visited the Lymans when preaching there in 1827, and had written to Charles: "I live now at Judge Lyman's who has a monopoly of the hospitality of the town."

Page 34

"Aunt Mary": Mary Moody Emerson. See note on page 172.

"Aunty Washburn," Mrs. Abiel Washburn, Jr., was Paulina Tucker, youngest sister of Ellen's father Bezaleel, and she was living in Boston at this time.

NOTES

"Mr Breed." Mr. and Mrs. Stephen P. Breed apparently took people in as boarders. An acquaintance of R.W.E.'s, John Farmer, lived with the Breeds when he was in Concord.

Page 35
Elizabeth Sparhawk had apparently just broken off her engagement, to the distress of her parents. Ellen is reminded of Lady Anne Lindsay's *Auld Robin Gray*:

> Auld Robin argued sair, though my mither didna speak.
> She looked in my face till my heart was like to break;
> So they gied him my hand, though my heart was at the sea,
> And auld Robin Gray is a gudeman to me.

Letter 9. Postmarked: Concord N.H. May 27.

Page 36
"Mr Adams." R.W.E. was living at Mr. Abel Adams', Chardon Street, Boston.

"the Monday in Jan." Ellen became ill in Boston in January, probably on Monday the nineteenth. R.W.E. wrote to William on January 28, 1829: "My beautiful friend has made me very sorry by being very ill & with that dangerous complaint which so often attacks the fairest in our stern climate. She has raised blood a week ago & I have been one of her nurses most unskilful but most interested & am writing my letter in her chamber. Beauty has got better & so I am better."

"Brown's Philosophy": *Lectures on the Philosophy of the Human Mind* by Thomas Brown, professor of moral philosophy at Edinburgh, published in 1820. There had been a Boston edition in 1826.

Page 37
The "Morrocco case" contained R.W.E.'s miniature, see note to Letter 3.

Mary Jane Kent, one of the Concord household, was the next to the youngest of Colonel Kent's children. She was born in 1806.

NOTES

Page 38

John Farmer, an authority on local history and genealogy, was an acquaintance of R.W.E.'s and corresponded with him about the early history of the Emerson family. He wrote *A Genealogical Register of the First Settlers of New England,* and was active in the establishment of the New Hampshire Historical Society.

"Scougal's Life of God": *The Life of God in the Soul of Man (or the Nature and Excellency of the Christian Religion),* written by Henry Scougal in 1677 and often reprinted.

Page 39

Letter *10*. Postmarked: Concord N.H. June 1.

Page 41

"an exchange with our Parson." If R.W.E. took over Mr. Moses Thomas' preaching for a Sunday, in Concord, Mr. Thomas would be free to preach at Portsmouth for Mr. Parker, the Unitarian minister there.

Page 42

"tempest." R.W.E. was reading Shakespeare during this period so that his "tempest" is likely to be the play. Ellen does not seem to have read any Shakespeare, and hers may be the poem by Sir Humphry Davy.

Mr. Harvey Courser has not been identified. The books were Izaak Walton's *The Compleat Angler* (1653), and Robert Pollok's *The Course of Time* (Edinburgh, 1827).

Page 43

Letter *11*. This letter was apparently carried to Boston by Hamilton Hutchins, enclosed in a letter to Aunt Washburn who lived in Boston. This is explained at the end of Ellen's letter.

Page 44

"Lady Grant" was Miss Zilpah Polly Grant, who ran the Adams Female Academy in Londonderry, New Hampshire,

NOTES

from 1824 to 1828. Ellen had been one of her pupils. Miss Mary Lyon also taught there, and both of these teachers had been pupils of R.W.E.'s second-cousin, the Reverend Joseph Emerson (see note to Letter 42). In Ellen's early notebook (Houghton 158a), "Londonderry" is written at the head of the first page, and is followed by the quotation from Allan Cunningham:

> 'Tis hame, hame where I wad be
> Hame, hame to my ain countrie.

A typically school-girlish poem follows. The page is torn off at the bottom. "Zippan" is apparently an adaptation of "Zilpah":

> There's Miss Grant   Oh Zippan Polly
> 'Twould be weak and childish folly
> To attempt to paint thee well
> Or thy fascination tell.

> Eyes of tiger furious glow
> All thy venom well I know
> Oft I raised my desk's thick cover
> Till their venom darts passed over.

> Yet I bless thee Lady Grant
> And forget it soon I shant
> However thy rage may be
> Never does it rest on me —

> Een across thy features grim
> I have traced a smile — but dim
> As the moon through wintry clouds . . .

Folded into another notebook is an undated letter to Miss Grant, which may have been a first draft, or never sent. Ellen tells Miss Grant that although their relation was short "the remembrance of it is among my pleasantest thoughts." She sends respects to Miss Lyon, love to her former schoolmates, and inquires about the school, as she has a cousin whom she would like to place under Miss Grant's care. This cousin may

NOTES

have been Elizabeth Tucker, younger daughter of Ellen's uncle Alanson, who was at "Derry Academy" according to R.W.E.'s journal in November 1831.

The "purple guard" was a watch-guard, a hand-made watch-chain of some sort.

Page 45

Washington Irving's *Life and Voyages of Christopher Columbus* was published in 1828, and *Chronicle of the Conquest of Granada* in 1829.

"Chaplain." R.W.E. had been appointed as chaplain to the state senate. This apparently had no political significance.

Page 46

Hamilton Hutchins, a graduate of Dartmouth, lived in Concord and was at this time studying for the bar.

Page 47

"I need not hide beneath my vest . . ." This poem is in Emerson's poetry notebook P, Houghton 136. One verse at the beginning was completely crossed out; it may have begun "Dear Heart"; the rest is given here as written in the notebook. R.W.E. published it with the title "Thine Eyes still Shined," and used only verses 2, 5, and 6. The Houghton Mifflin edition of the poems in 1904 added verses 3, 4, and 7 in a note. The present first verse seems not to have been published.

Page 49

Letter *12*. Postmarked: Concord N.H. June 8.

Page 50

The quotation is from Dryden's paraphrase of the twenty-ninth ode of the third book of Horace. It is quoted in Dr. Johnson's *The Rambler*, No. 41, and Ellen may have seen it there.

> Happy the man, and happy he alone,
> He, who can call to-day his own:
> He who, secure within, can say,

NOTES

To-morrow do thy worst, for I have liv'd to-day;
  Be fair, or foul, or rain, or shine,
The joys I have possess'd, in spite of fate are mine,
  Not Heaven itself upon the past has power;
But what has been, has been, and I have had my hour.

"light fantastic horse-shoe": The reference is to the line from John Milton's *Allegro*:

Come and trip it as you go
On the light fantastic toe . . .

Page 52

"Mr. Lathrop" is probably the minister from Dover, New Hampshire, who preached in Concord occasionally.

The Reverend Nathaniel Bouton had been minister at the old North Church since 1825. This was his second marriage, his first wife having died suddenly the preceding year. Mr. Bouton wrote a history of Concord and a number of articles on antiquarian and historical subjects.

"Betty Jackson." The only way to explain this reference, and the later ones, is to assume that "Betty" is Ellen's nickname for Dr. Jackson. Perhaps she considered him too fussy. "Forgive," written below the name, would be Ellen's apology to her doctor for calling him a "Betty."

Letter 13. Postmarked: Concord N.H. June 11.

Page 53

Letter 14. This letter was written on Saturday, June 13, and carried to Boston by "Mercury," who may have been Colonel Kent. The corner of the letter is completely torn off along the folds.

Page 54

George, Colonel Kent's second son, had graduated from Dartmouth in 1814. He was married, practiced law in Concord, and was active in town affairs.

NOTES

R.W.E. kept a record of his preaching from October 1826 on, writing down where he preached and which sermons he used. This record is Houghton 96.

Letter 15. Postmarked: Concord N.H. July 3.

Page 56

"Cousin Susan T" was Susan Tucker, Ellen's first cousin, daughter of her uncle Alanson.

The quotation is from Sir Walter Scott's *Lochinvar*:
"I long wooed your daughter, my suit you denied,
Love swells like the Solway, but ebbs like its tide."

Page 58

In Ellen's copy of *Sabbath Recreations* (see note to Letter 19) there is a bookmark at Robert Southey's lines on Love, which she quoted (the passage is from *The Curse of Kehama*):

They sin who tell us Love can die:
With life all other passions fly, . . .
But Love is indestructible
Its holy flame for ever burneth,
From heaven it came, to heaven returneth;
Too oft on earth a troubled guest,
At times deceived, at times oppress'd,
It is here tried and purified,
Then hath in heaven its perfect rest;
It soweth here with toil and care,
But the harvest-time of Love is there.

Letter 16. Probably written on Saturday, July 4, and carried to Boston by "Mr John Gardner," whose name is written on the outside of the letter below R.W.E.'s name and address.

Letter 17. Written on Sunday, July 5, and also taken to Boston by Mr. Gardner. "Mr John Gardener" is written on the outside.

Page 60

The quotation is from *The Pleasures of Hope* by Thomas Campbell:

NOTES

Why do those cliffs of shadowy tint appear
More sweet than all the landscape smiling near? —
'Tis distance lends enchantment to the view,
And robes the mountain in its azure hue.

Page 61
"Harvey," to judge from the references to him, was Colonel Kent's hired man, one of whose duties was to collect the mail from the post-office. Rosanna, Sally, and Eliza are not mentioned elsewhere, and could have been servants or nurses — or family pets.

Page 61
Letter 18. Postmarked: Concord N.H. July 6.

Page 62
The expression "purple wings" may have come from Milton's verses quoted in *The Rambler*, No. 86:
Here love his golden shafts employs, here lights
His constant lamp, and waves his purple wings,
Reigns here, and revels . . .
"that St. Augustine poem." R.W.E. had visited St. Augustine, Florida, in February 1827. He wrote a number of poems in his journals while he was there, and Ellen must be referring to one of them.

Anne of Geierstein; or The Maiden of the Mist, by Sir Walter Scott, was published in 1829.

Page 63
Letter 19. Postmarked: Concord N.H. July 8.

Page 64
"Sab Recreations": *Sabbath Recreations, or Select Poetry of a Religious Kind*, first American edition by John Pierpont (Boston, 1829). Ellen's copy has her name written in it in R.W.E.'s handwriting. The poem referred to is by Mrs H. Tighe, and is called "The Lily, an Emblem of Christian Hope."

NOTES

How wither'd, faded, seems the form
Of yon obscure unsightly root!
Yet from the blight of winter's storm
It hides secure the precious root.

The careless eye can find no grace,
No beauty in the scaly folds;
Nor see, within the dark embrace,
What latent loveliness it holds.

Yet in that bulb, those sapless scales,
The lily wraps her silver vest,
Till vernal suns and vernal gales
Shall kiss once more her fragrant breast.
. . .
Sweet smile of Hope! delicious tear!
The sun, the shower indeed *shall* come;
The promised verdant shoot appear,
And nature bid her blossom bloom,

And thou, O virgin queen of spring,
Shall, from thy dark and lowly bed,
Bursting thy green sheath's silken string,
Unveil thy charms, thy perfume shed; . . .
[There are six more verses.]

Page 65
   Letter 20. Postmarked: Concord N.H. July [ ]; written Friday July 10.

Page 66
   The "Shaker Village" was located in Canterbury, New Hampshire, about ten miles north of Concord.
   The quotation is from the first verse of *Ballad Stanzas* by Thomas Moore:
   I knew by the smoke, that so gracefully curl'd
   Above the green elms, that a cottage was near,
   And I said, "If there's peace to be found in the world
   The heart that was humble might hope for it here!"

NOTES

Page 68
Letter 21. Postmarked: Concord N.H. July 13.

Ellen is referring to *The Castle of Indolence* by James Thomson (1748).

"ninety and nine." Matthew 18.12: "How think ye? if a man have an hundred sheep, and one of them be gone astray, doth he not leave the ninety and nine, and goeth into the mountains, and seeketh that which is gone astray?" On July 18, R.W.E. wrote to his brother William: "I am going to Concord N.H. next week if I can steal away, for Ellen says I must leave my ninety & nine & come & hunt my stray sheep in the wilderness. Wo is me my brother that sickness & sorrow steal into the fold of this world & prey on what is preciousest." For Ellen's poem on this subject see p. 154.

Page 69
"Mr & Mrs Thomas." The Reverend Moses Thomas and Mary Jane Kent had apparently just become engaged; see below.

Philip Carrigain was a Concord lawyer, active in the town, a witty man and a good speaker, who had written both prose and verse.

"water of oblivion." One wonders if Moses Thomas had been one of Ellen's beaux. It would explain her suggestion of forgetting the past.

Page 70
"pris'ners of hope" seems to be another of Ellen's many Biblical allusions (Zechariah 9.12).

Page 71
"Anne of the Mist" is Scott's *Anne of Geierstein*.

Letter 22. Postmarked: Concord N.H. July [ ]; written Monday July 20.

NOTES

Page 72
"Cousin Alanson" was Ellen's first cousin, Susan Tucker's brother.

Page 73
"resemblance of her cousin George." The reference must be to a fancied resemblance between Ellen's brother George, who had died in 1825, and R.W.E.

Letter 23. Postmarked: Concord N.H. July [ ]; probably written on July 23 or 24.

Page 74
"Bro George." A newspaper clipping in Ellen's copybook (Houghton 157) gives the following account of George Tucker:

> In one of Mr Carter's Letters from Europe describing his visit to the Cemetery of Pere LaChaise in Paris, he speaks of seeing the graves of Lieutenant Richards & Mr Tucker, two young Americans who died and were buried on the same day. . . . Mr George W. Tucker received part of his classical education at Yale College & afterward pursued the study of physic in Boston. His health failing him he sailed on a voyage to France with the flattering, but delusive, hope that a milder climate might conduce to its restoration. He survived his arrival in Paris only about three months and died in October 1825 at the age of twenty-two.

Two poems follow — the "Fare-well," apparently written by him on the eve of his departure for France and later found among his papers, and a poem "To the memory of Professor Fisher of Yale College who was lost in the sloop Albion on her passage from New York to Liverpool in 1823." The "Farewell" is untitled and not dedicated to anyone, but according to this article "his Mother is the one to whom his thoughts were then directed":

> Why tell me that the owlet's scream
> Is heard from yonder mould'ring tree?

NOTES

Why tell me that the rising blast
Mourns fearful o'er the misty sea?
I heed them not. The owl but screams
His welcome to the stormy night;
And the storm blast that frights thee so,
Rushes to end my bounding flight.
Through the dull gloom there shines a star
That guides me to another clime;
It is the beacon fire of Hope,
Fanned by the glowing wing of Time.
I've wove a web – O break it not,
E'en if its tissue be a dream,
O drive not fancy from her throne,
E'en if she sits in falsehood's beam.
O, if the gem of earthly bliss,
Bright Health, illumes mine eyes no more,
Say not 'tis all in vain I seek
Its sparkle on a distant shore.
Adieu. The tear that fills thine eye
Another beacon-light shall be –
Here in my heart I bid it live
To guide me back to home and thee.

George kept a journal briefly describing his trip to Paris, his daily life, activities, reading and expenses. This was his last entry: "Vendredi Aout douzieme – Pleasant and unpleasant – wrote home by Dennison. Have taken a horrid cold which has turned my blood to melted lead – Expendit 25 . 3 sous." Ellen later took over the journal to use for one of her notebooks. She wrote: "This is George's book his latest thoughts written out — I take the book but the blank leaves between our effusions are emblematic of the blank that stops me when my thoughts would follow him – oh whither? Oh whither!!! — The other [her sister Mary] – her footsteps were traced in light – her destination ever glowed in her eye – her body died and her spirit which had so long almost been

NOTES

heard to flutter against its decayed house stretched its impatient wings for Heaven – and disappeared
 "Why then their loss deplore who are not lost"
 [The quotation is from Young's *Night Thoughts*.]

Page 75
 Letter *24*. Postmarked: Concord N.H. July [ ]; probably written over the week-end and mailed on Monday July 27.

Page 76
 Letter *25*. Postmarked: Concord N.H. July [ ]; written on Monday July 27, and probably mailed the following day.

Page 77
 Rebecca was the youngest of Colonel Kent's children.

 Henry Cheever Pratt was a portrait and landscape painter, a pupil of S. F. B. Morse, who had come from New Hampshire originally and at this time had a studio in Boston. A critic commented that Pratt "aimed to please, and was not bad enough to be a primitive, and not good enough to be great."

 "*Sir*" is another of Ellen's names for her stepfather, Colonel Kent.

Page 79
 "Willis's periodical" is probably a reference to the *Youth's Companion*, a magazine started in 1828 by Nathaniel Willis.

 Letter *26*. Postmarked: Concord N.H. July [ ]; written on Tuesday July 28.

 Miss Alice Bacon ran a boarding-house at 7 Suffolk Place, Boston.

Page 80
 "Grandma Tucker" was Hannah Jedidah Warren Tucker, daughter of Deacon Warren of Middleboro, mother of Bezaleel, Alanson, Serena Hubbard, Paulina Washburn, and seven other children. She had four portraits painted as gifts to her children. This was one of them.

NOTES

Letter 27. Postmarked: Concord N.H. July 30.

Page 81

"Oft in the stilly night" was quoted by Ellen from Thomas Moore's song:

> Oft in the stilly night
> Ere slumber's chain has bound me,
> Fond memory brings the light
> Of other days around me.

"Canterbury" was an area in Roxbury, a rocky and wooded section now included in Franklin Park. Ruth Emerson had moved there with her sons in 1823, and lived there for several years. R.W.E. describes this visit in a letter to William, July 27: "Last Saturday Chas & I went to Canterbury – tied our horse at ye old barn & played gipsy in all the old pastures identified ye old localities & eat up ye sons or great grandsons of ye old berries. I hope to live there again yet." Ellen's old home was the Sumner house on the Dedham turnpike in Roxbury, where she lived before her father's death.

Page 82

George Adams Sampson was a friend of R.W.E.'s and a member of the Second Church in Boston.

Page 83

"Byron" was a spaniel, to whom Ellen had written a poem about 1825, beginning:

> Byron   tell me spaniel why
> Why the sparkle in your eye –
> Hast thou missed my wandering feet
> Missed me at my well-known seat?

"Felicia" is not mentioned elsewhere, but may have been the canary mourned by Ellen in a long series of verses beginning:

> The Eastern wind blows blue and shrill
> The pelting rain is falling still
> And nature's moans from tree to tree
> Are echoed with wild sympathy,

NOTES

And where art thou, my little one,
My pet, my nursling in the storm
Hast thou a shelter where to run
A nest to keep thy bosom warm

O is thy soft and golden wing
Still beating gainst the furious blast
Poor youthful inexperienced thing
I fear this day may prove they last.

Page 84
  Letter 28. This letter was written on Thursday July 30, and carried to Boston by Colonel Kent. Ellen wrote on the outside: "Fav by Col Wm A Kent." According to the endorsement, R.W.E. received it on Saturday, August 1.

Page 85
  Letter 29. There is no postmark, nor any indication that someone carried it to Boston. It was written August 3 or 4, and probably sent by the stage.

Page 86
  Letter 30. Postmarked: Concord N.H. Aug [ ]; written on Thursday August 20. R.W.E. had left for Boston the day before.

Page 87
  Mr. Pliny Cutler was the executor of Beza Tucker's estate, and Ellen's guardian. It can be assumed that there were legal transactions in connection with her estate to be attended to before her marriage, probably also the making of her will, etc., that she did not enjoy having to discuss.

Page 88
  Letter 31. Postmarked: Concord N.H. Aug [ ]; written on Saturday August 22.

  "that little helm" is an allusion to the passage in James 3: "Behold also the ships, which though they be so great, and are driven of fierce winds, yet are they turned about with a

NOTES

very small helm, whithersoever the governor listeth. Even so the tongue is a little member and boasteth great things."

"chill confident." See the poem on p. 156 — "I chided the moon, she was icy cold – "

Page 90
Letter 32. Postmarked: Concord N.H. Aug 25.

"Mrs K" was Mrs. Hannah Keating, who took in boarders at her house in Chardon Street, Boston.

Page 91
"*last end* of that toy." Ellen was thinking of a phrase from Luke 11:26: "and the last state of that man is worse then the first."

"For under that black veil a darker veil . . ." Ellen may possibly be paraphrasing the lines from Milton's *Paradise Lost*, Book 4, which run:

And in the lowest deep, a lower deep
Still threatening to devour me opens wide.

"sour converse" is a reference to a poem in R.W.E.'s journal, June 1827, called "At the Old Manse":

And hark! where overhead the ancient crows
Hold their sour conversation in the sky.

Page 92
"my love forever burneth From heaven it came to heaven returneth" was quoted from the verses on Love by Southey; see note on Letter 15.

Letter 33. Postmarked: Concord N.H. Aug 28.

Page 93
Ellen had two cousins named Mary, both of whom were younger than she was: her Aunt Serena Hubbard's daughter Mary Ann, and her Aunt Paulina Washburn's daughter Mary.

"bid the 'proud world Goodbye' " is a reference to R.W.E.'s poem called "Good-bye," which begins:

NOTES

"Good-bye, proud world! I'm going home:
Thou art not my friend, and I'm not thine."

Page 95
   Letter 34. Postmarked: Concord N.H. Aug 31.

The letter mentioned here may have been about setting the date of the wedding. This would have been something that R.W.E. would have had to arrange with Colonel Kent. It seems that Colonel Kent did not expect the wedding to take place till spring, but that Ellen and R.W.E. wanted it earlier. A reference in the preceding letter indicates arrangements to be made

Page 97
   Letter 35. Postmarked: Concord N.H. Sept 4.

Page 101
"Dear Ellen" and "I call her beautiful." These poems, with the notation "1829, September. Pepperell," occur in R.W.E.'s journal, Houghton 19. Since there is no record that R.W.E. preached at Pepperell in September, and since it is on one route between Concord, New Hampshire, and Worcester, Massachusetts, it seems logical to guess that he stopped there on the trip with Ellen, her mother, and Margaret, between September 8 and 16. The conversational tone of the poems indicates that he and Ellen were together at the time.

Page 103
   Letter 36. Postmarked: Concord N.H. Sep. 18.

"The Last Man" and "The Rainbow" are by Thomas Campbell, whose *Poetical Works* were published in 1828.

Letter 37. There is no postmark. Ellen said at the end of the letter: "I shall send by the stage." It was probably written Monday, September 21.

Page 104
"the publishment" may refer to the wedding announcement.

NOTES

The date of the wedding had doubtless been set during R.W.E.'s visit, when the family were together.

"a clock like the one Mrs H. sings of" refers to a poem by Mrs. Hemans called "The Dial of Flowers," which begins:

'Twas a lovely thought to mark the hours
As they floated in light away,
By the opening and the folding flowers,
That laugh to the summer's day.

Page 105
   Letter 38. Postmarked Concord N.H. Sep. 25.
   "Byron" is the spaniel; see note on Letter 27.

Page 111
   Aunt Mary's letter was addressed to "Mr R. Waldo Emerson, Cambridge, Mss." and was dated on the outside "Waterford Me Jan 8th." It was sent by the stage, as explained in a postscript to R.W.E. The endorsement is in R.W.E.'s writing, "M M E to Ellen Jan 1829." The specific works recommended for Ellen's reading were *A Serious Call to a Devout and Holy Life, Adapted to the State and Condition of All Orders of Christians*, by William Law (1728) — R.W.E.'s own copy of this book was published in Boston in 1818 — and *The Complaint, or Night Thoughts on Life, Death and Immortality*, by Edward Young (1774). Aunt Mary's heroines were Flora MacIvor in *Waverley* and Jeanie Deans in *Heart of Midlothian*, novels by Sir Walter Scott, and Mme. de Stael's *Corinne*. "Moore's" heroine has not been identified, as Aunt Mary's writing is not good, nor her spelling always correct.

Page 112
   Letter 39. There is no postmark; the contents place it in December 1829.

Page 114
   "And, Ellen, when the greybeard years." These verses are in the Blotting Book Y, Houghton 22.

NOTES

Page 115

The Philadelphia Journal. The first four lines are quoted from Mrs Hemans' "The Hour of Death," the fourth verse of which runs as follows:

> Youth and the opening rose
> May look like things too glorious for decay,
> And smile at thee; but thou art not of those
> Who wait the ripen'd bloom to seize their prey.

"A boat, a boat" is a well-known round.

Page 124

Letter 41. William Henry Furness had been a good friend of R.W.E.'s ever since they went to school together as small boys in Boston. He was a Unitarian minister in Philadelphia. Thomas Sully, a pupil of Benjamin West's, was a well-known painter of portraits and historical scenes.

Letter 42. Postmarked: New York Apr 1; written in Philadelphia on March 28, 1830, and endorsed by M.M.E.: "Ellen from Philadelphia." It is addressed to "Miss M.M.Emerson care of Rev Joseph Emerson, Wethersfield, Conn." Joseph Emerson, minister and schoolteacher, was the son of M.M.E.'s first cousin Daniel. According to *The Ipswich Emersons* (Boston, 1900), "he was interested in education generally, and especially in the education of women . . . His school was the first advanced school for girls. Mary Lyon, who founded South Hadley Seminary [later Mount Holyoke], and Miss Grant, the founder of Ipswich Academy, were his pupils."

Page 125

Dr. Philip Doddridge was an important writer in the eighteenth-century Unitarian movement, and wrote *The Rise and Progress of Religion in the Soul* (1745), and other religious works and a volume of hymns. R.W.E. says of Dr. Doddridge in his journal (February 1828) that he "owed all his fame to his getting up at five o'clock every morning and writing for two hours what everybody knew and said before."

NOTES

Page 126

The "Golden Rule" sermon was R.W.E.'s sermon 65, with the text "And as ye would that men should do to you, do ye also to them likewise." This sermon had been preached four times in Boston and Cambridge.

Page 127

"I am alone . . ." R.W.E. copied this poem into the small verse-book, Houghton 197, where he had written down eighteen of Ellen's poems.

Page 128

Letter 43. No postmark; addressed to "Mr Edward B Emerson Care of Mr William Emerson No 30 Pine St NYork" It may have been carried by Mr. Farnsworth, whose name appears on the outside of the letter.

"Christ Rejected" was a very large oil painting by Benjamin West.

Page 130

"To E.T.E. at Philadelphia." This poem occurs in the notebook Houghton 136. It was published in the *Dial* in 1843 with the title "To Ellen at the South."

Page 132

Letter 44. This letter is addressed to "William Emerson Esq., Office No 60 Wall St. New York" and is postmarked "New York Aug 2." It is dated in R.W.E.'s writing, and endorsed by William, "Ellen & Waldo Emerson July 30/30." Edward was visiting William at the time.

Clarence by Catherine Maria Sedgewick was published in 1830.

Page 133

The quotation is from William Cullen Bryant's *The Old Man's Funeral*:

Ye sigh not when the sun his course fulfilled,
His glorious course, rejoicing earth and sky,

NOTES

> In the soft evening, when the winds are stilled,
> Sinks where his islands of refreshment lie,
> And leaves the smile of his departure spread
> O'er the warm-colored heaven and ruddy mountain head.

R.W.E. finished the letter, beginning his part, "How shall I dare come in the rear of – but it will not do for husband and wifey to compliment each other at their poor brothers' expense hungering for news."

Page 134
    Letter 45. Undated; written during the autumn of 1830.

Page 135
    Letter 46. Edward had been with William in New York for part of the summer and returned there in September, 1830. In November he became ill and was advised to go south for his health. He sailed for Santa Cruz in the West Indies on December 12 from New York.

Ellen was mixing up two of Robert Southey's wicked bishops — Bishop Bruno, in the poem of that name, and Bishop Hatto, in "God's Judgement on a Wicked Bishop," who was devoured by rats.

Page 136
    Letter 47. No postmark; no date.

"Aunt Hubbard" was Mrs Ahira Hubbard, Bezaleel Tucker's younger sister Serena. She had six children; two of the older ones were Henry and Harriet, the "2 Hs" mentioned below. It is confusing that Ellen referred to "uncle P" rather than to "uncle A."

Ellen's sister, Paulina Tucker, married Joshua Nash at about this time, and the reference must be to that event. The letters of the Tucker family do not seem to have survived, and this is Ellen's only mention of it.

NOTES

Page 137
Letter 48. Postmarked: Boston Ms Jan 13. "Kindness of E. Fuller Esq" is written on the outside. The letter was written the evening of January 12, 1831.

R.W.E.'s sermon on January 12, 1831 was preached to the Howard Benevolent Society at the Old South Church. It was Sermon 104, and was entitled "Self and Others." The New Years Eve sermon was entitled "How Old art Thou?" and was Sermon 101.

Page 138
"Grandfather" was Dr. Ezra Ripley of Concord, Massachusetts, R.W.E.'s step-grandfather, who lived at the Old Manse.

Page 139
The letters of William, Charles, and Edward Emerson are unpublished. They are the property of the R.W.E. Memorial Association. Charles' letters to Aunt Mary are addressed to her at Dr. Ripley's in Concord, Massachusetts.

"Margaret." When Margaret Tucker died, R.W.E. wrote in his journal on November 24, 1832: "Farewell to thee for a little time, my kind and sympathizing sister. Go rejoice with Ellen, so lately lost, in God's free and glorious universe. Tell her, if she needs to be told, how dearly she is remembered, how dearly valued. Rejoice together that you are free of your painful corporeal imprisonment. I may well mourn your loss, for in many sour days I had realized the delicacy and sweetness of a sister's feeling. I had rejoiced too, as always, in the gifts of a true lady, in whom was never anything little or mean seen or suspected, who was all gentleness, purity and sense with a rare elevation of sentiments. God comfort the bitter lonely hours which the sorrowing mother must spend here.

"Farewell, dear girl. I have a very narrow acquaintance, and of it you have been a large part. We anchor upon a few, and you have had the character and dignity that promised every-

NOTES

thing to the esteem and affection of years. Think kindly of me, — I know you will, — but perchance the disembodied can do much more, can elevate the sinking spirit and purify and urge it to generous purposes. Teach me to make trifles, trifles, and work with consistency and in earnest to my true ends. The only sister I ever had, pass on, pure soul! to the opening heaven."

Mrs. Kent died in the spring of 1833, and R.W.E. wrote in his journal while staying in Florence, Italy, on May 8th: "To-day I heard, by Charles's letter, of the death of Ellen's mother. Fast, fast the bonds dissolve that I was so glad to wear. She has been a most kind and exemplary mother, and how painfully disappointed! Happy now. And oh, what events and thoughts in which I should have deepest sympathy does this thin partition of flesh entirely hide! Does the heart in that world forget the heart that did beat with it in this? Do jealousies, do fears, does the observation of faults, intervene? Dearest friends, I would be loved by all of you: dearest friend! we shall meet again."

Page 140

"There is one birth . . ." These words occur in a passage in R.W.E.'s Blotting Book ψ, Houghton 24, dated February 13, 1831. The descriptions of Ellen are chosen from among the many references to her in R.W.E.'s journals during the five years following her death.

Page 141

The last quoted passage about Ellen was written by R.W.E. in his journal in February 1839 (Houghton 36).

Page 142

"Dost thou not hear me" and "Dust unto Dust." These poems occur in the Blotting Book, Houghton 24. A group of poems is set into the main body of the journal, all apparently written soon after Ellen's death.

NOTES

THE POEMS

Page 147

R.W.E.'s notebook of Ellen's verses is Houghton 197.

Page 149

"The Violet." William Cullen Bryant's "The Death of the Flowers," written after the death of his sister, in 1825, seems to have influenced Ellen's poem. In a letter to William in 1831, R.W.E. says: "The 'death of the Flowers' was meat & drink to my noble flower." R.W.E. published this poem in the *Dial*, January 1841.

Page 153

"Love scatters oil. . ." R.W.E. published this poem, with the title "Lines," in the first number of the *Dial*, July 1, 1840, with several minor changes of wording, considerable alteration in the fifth verse, and the substitution of the following last two lines for those of Ellen's:

Then a clear voice spoke
And my tears are dry.

Page 154

"Thou left'st thy ninety-nine to seek . . ." This poem was probably written when R.W.E. came to Concord early in August 1829. The reference to the ninety and nine occurs in Letter 21 (see note also).

Page 156

"I chided the moon . . ." The present first verse is numbered "2" as though Ellen had intended to have another verse before it. This is the last poem in R.W.E.'s collection of Ellen's verses.

Page 160

"How true! each hours researches prove . . ." This poem is written on the back of a note beginning: "Thank you, My Dear Mrs Emerson," and signed "S. A. Burditt." The note thanks Ellen for the loan of Herbert's poems and a sermon of

NOTES

R.W.E.'s. It can be dated late in 1829 or in 1830. The note was tucked into Ellen's Album.

Page 161
"I am the grave's . . ." This fragment is to be found in "George's" notebook.

"And Hope, sweet bird . . ." These last lines are written in pencil in "George's" notebook.

THE NOTEBOOKS

Page 162
The notebooks are Houghton 157, 158a, and 159 respectively.

Page 166
The album is held by the R.W.E. Memorial Association.

Notes on the Text

The letters were written in black ink on double sheets of paper, 8" × 9¾". The sheets were then folded in three lengthwise, in three again to form an envelope, and sealed with red sealing wax. The seal frequently tore off a piece of the paper when the letter was opened. Ends of letters and postscripts were written across the ends of the outside sheet which would be folded under. The damage to the edges and folds of the letters can be explained by their narrow escape from burning in the fire at the Emerson house in 1872. Most of the letters are charred along the edges, and blurred in places by the water used to put out the fire.

The letters have been copied as they were written. The original spelling has been retained, — "ryhmes," "recieve," "sheperd" etc — and the original punctuation. Ellen used dashes of varying lengths for most of her punctuation. In the early letters particularly she read over what she had written and added comments and explanations. These were written along the sides of the sheets or between the lines. Groups of words were occasionally bracketed together with a lightly drawn circle or oval. In printing the letters it has not always been possible to follow Ellen's arrangement of words exactly, and these exceptions are explained in the following notes. Where the paper has been torn or damaged, so that the words are illegible or missing, substitutions have been made in square brackets to give the approximate sense of the original.

The page and line are listed below for each place where the arrangement of words in print differs from that in the original.

11|1   The endorsement is written on the outside, and above it in a lightly sketched square is 'I letter.'

NOTES ON THE TEXT

12| 6   "Oh the metaphorical droppings of a girl in her teens" is written in above "have chilled the swift flowing fount."

12|29   "very clearly expressed" is written in, without parentheses, at the end of the preceding sentence.

13|17   "verily like the shadow of my own when the sun is low" is written along the side of the sheet.

14|15   "matronly reflections" is written along the side of the sheet.

21|21   "dear Waldo" is written below "and truly am I yours" and a line is drawn around the two phrases.

22|6   "any thing" is interlineated above "every thing."

28|14   A piece of paper is torn away by the seal.

29|3   The last sentence is written in as a postscript across the top of the first sheet.

32|17   "not rightly" is interlineated above "wrongly."

35|8   The last paragraph of the letter is written at the head of the first sheet.

36|5   Ellen wrote the explanation "this word is stirred" with a line around it below her original "stirred," which was written illegibly.

39|4   The postscript was written on the outside of the letter.

42|1   "*Grandma forgets to modernize herself — risk" is written in at the bottom of the sheet. Ellen used the asterisk here.

42|18   A very small piece of the paper is torn away by the seal.

43|1   The last paragraph was written on the outside of the letter.

44|18   "beautiful perspicuity" is written in below the word "remember."

46|4   Ellen wrote "in quality" above and "in quantity" below the words "how much" and encircled the six words.

46|10   A piece of paper was torn away by the seal.

46|29   On the outside of the sheet, near a tear in the paper, is written: "It is all owing to the weakness of the paper — not a bit to my clumsiness."

50|18   Ellen wrote "*a fib*" above "with me" and drew a circle around the words.

51|4   "expressive," with a line around it, is written below the words "*thin as air.*"

NOTES ON THE TEXT

51|26	The edge of the paper is torn off, leaving only the "q" of "quality."
52|3	"soft kisses" with an oval drawn around it was inserted above "bright rays."
52|8	"presumptuous" is written below "*be mine* eternally" and a bracket is drawn around it.
52|13	"Forgive" is written with a bracket under the words "Betty Jackson."
53|26ff.	The corner is missing where the paper tore off along the folds. The words in brackets have been substituted to indicate the general sense. The tail of the letter "g" is visible to make the word "bag" seem reasonable.
56|22	Ellen began the letter "Dearest Waldo" and then crossed out "est Waldo" and wrote "Friend" instead.
56|29	"un" was written above the line just before "successfully."
57|11ff.	The seal tore away a piece of the paper, but the missing words are obvious.
57–58	The last section of the letter is written in two parts across the ends of the outside sheet. The upper lines in both cases are rubbed, and blurred by charring and water (at the time of the fire in the Emerson house, 1872).
58|16	"The pills arrived" was written by Ellen in pencil at the beginning of Paulina's letter.
	A message was written along the side of the paper but was completely erased.
65|6	"3 weeks ago" is written above "last week."
67|29	The end of the letter from "wait a giff" on was written across one end of the outside sheet, and the postscript across the other end.
70|27	There is a simple pair of quotation marks after "skin" which has been omitted here.
78|24	Ellen first wrote "sentiment so stirring of the songs." She then put a "2" under "sentiment" and "one" under "stirring."
80|21	The postscript was written by itself on an inside sheet.
80|24	Above the poem in the center of the sheet is a small pencil sketch of a little man sitting on one end of a seesaw, with a heavy sack holding down the other end. Below

NOTES ON THE TEXT

	the picture is written 'Alas poor Cupid," and above it, blurred at the edge, is "This is a [ ] too."
83|11	A piece of paper is torn off by the seal.
83|27	The last sentence was written along the side of the first page of the letter, opposite the poem.
85|3	Ellen wrote "the spirit departing from" and then wrote "out of" on top of "from."
93|5	Ellen omitted the quotation marks after "phiz."
93|11	"our" is written closely above "my."
94|11	"*better half*" is enclosed in a slightly drawn square.
96|5	"chills" was written in just above "numbs."
99|28	The seal has torn away a piece of the paper.
100|10	The last sentence was added on the outside of the letter.
106|7	"leanly" was written before "scantily" and had a circle drawn around it.
107|8	The last paragraph was written on the opposite page to mask the end of the letter. The seal tore away a piece of the paper.
124|16	Ellen interlineated "makes" above "gives."

Index

Adams, Abel, 18, 36, 100, 123, 179
Bacon, Alice, 79, 190
Birch, Mrs., 14
Bouton, Nathaniel, 52, 183
Breed, Stephen, 34, 179
Burditt, S. A., 201

Carrigain, Philip, 69, 187
Carter, Professor, 94
Chandler, Mrs. Abel, 31, 42, 178
Cole, Mr., 14
Courser, Harvey, 42, 180
Cutler, Pliny, 87, 90, 94, 192

Emerson, Charles Chauncy, 5, 6, 44, 112, 115, 123, 133, 136, 137, 139, 171, 199
Emerson, Edward Bliss, 1, 6, 15, 44, 89, 112, 113, 128, 135, 139, 171, 197, 198, 199
Emerson, Edward Waldo, v, 172
Emerson, Joseph, 181, 196
Emerson, Mary Moody, 5, 6, 34, 60, 105, 111, 112, 115, 124, 128, 136, 137, 139, 171–173, 195, 199
Emerson, Ruth Haskins, 6, 44, 132, 134, 172, 191
Emerson, William, 1, 5, 6, 89, 92, 98, 113, 128, 132, 171, 197, and passim

Farmer, John, 38, 42, 179, 180
Forbes, Edith Emerson, v, viii, 176
Furness, Mr. & Mrs. William Henry, 124, 126, 196

Goodridge, Sarah, 37, 43, 175–176
Grant, Zilpah Polly, 44, 163, 180–181, 196

Harvey, 61, 85, 88, 185
Hubbard, Mrs. Ahira (Serena Tucker), 136, 190, 193, 198
Hutchins, Hamilton, 46, 180, 182

Jackson, Dr. James, 20, 52, 60, 61, 174, 183
Jackson, Lydia, viii, 140, 176

Kast, Mrs. Thomas (Hannah Haskins), 177
Keating, Hannah, 90, 104, 111, 193
Kent, Edward, 4, 15, 173
Kent, George, 4, 54, 172, 183
Kent, Margaret Tucker, 2, 34, 46, 69, 70, 77, 78, 79, 86, 100, 136, 163, 200, and passim
Kent, Mary Jane, 4, 37, 45, 51, 61, 74, 77, 95, 98, 179, 187
Kent, Rebecca, 4, 77, 94, 190
Kent, William, 4, 172
Kent, William Austin, 2, 4, 34, 41, 58, 61, 63, 74, 77, 78, 91, 94, 95, 99, 111, 166, 171–172, 194, and passim

Lathrop, Mr., 52, 104, 183
Lobdell, Mrs., 66
Lovejoy, 37
Lyman, Mrs. Joseph, 33, 57, 86, 178
Lyon, Mary, 181, 196

INDEX

MacElroy, Mrs., 122
Mellen, Charlotte, 171
Mellen, Eliza, 66
Meserve, Mr. & Mrs., 106

Nash, Joshua, 198

Parker, Mr., 42, 180
Perry, Mrs., 132
Pratt, Henry Cheever, 77, 190

Ripley, Ezra, 6, 138, 199
Ripley, Phebe, 6

Sampson, George Adams, 82, 191
Shepard, Mr. & Mrs. George, 29, 177
Sparhawk, Elizabeth, 15, 35, 38, 50, 54, 70, 99, 173, 179
Sudwitz, 55
Sully, Thomas, 124, 196

Thomas, Moses, 32, 34, 37, 38, 41, 45, 53, 69, 178, 180, 187
Tomlinson, Gideon, 27, 177
Tucker, Alanson, 72, 74, 188

Tucker, Bezaleel, 2, 140, 171, 191, 192
Tucker, Elizabeth, 182
Tucker, George, 2, 73, 74, 147, 163, 168, 188–189
Tucker, Margaret, 2, 4, 34, 45, 50, 66, 72, 77, 85, 93, 95, 100, 105, 111, 115, 138, 199–200, and passim
Tucker, Mary, 2, 147, 189
Tucker, Mrs. Nathaniel (Hannah Jedidah Warren), 80, 171, 190
Tucker, Paulina, 2, 4, 34, 45, 50, 66, 77, 85, 95, 104, 107, 111, 198, and passim
Tucker, Susan, 56, 60, 64, 66, 70, 73, 74, 184
Turner, Mr., 125

Ware, Henry, 18, 20, 174
Washburn, Mrs. Abiel (Paulina Tucker), 34, 42, 46, 134, 168, 178, 190, 193
Weston, 14
Williams, John, 14, 20, 173